E=M

Creating new and better plants
LUTHER BURBANK

Britannica Bookshelf--Great Lives for Young Americans

Creating new and better plants

LUTHER BURBANK

by Paul Bacon

Illustrated by Dan Siculan

Published by
ENCYCLOPAEDIA BRITANNICA PRESS, Chicago

"And we make (by art) in the same orchards and gardens, trees and flowers to come earlier or later than their seasons; and to come up and bear more speedily than by their natural course they do. We make them also by art greater much than their nature; and their fruit greater and sweeter and of differing taste, smell, color, and figures, from their nature."

Francis Bacon, *The New Atlantis*, 1627

TABLE OF CONTENTS

INTRODUCTION

In the modern supermarket, long counters are heaped with fruits and vegetables. There are plums, pears, apples, oranges, grapes and peaches; peas, squash, lettuce, tomatoes and beans. Seventy-five years ago grocery stores looked very different, as different as the produce on their counters. These fruits and vegetables would look as old fashioned to us now as the stores themselves.

Gardens today produce big, white daisies, beautiful lilies, dahlias, gladioli, roses and poppies. These, too, are different from those you would have seen fifty to a hundred years ago.

It used to be that changes in fruits, flowers and vegetables were left up to nature, and each improvement was then cultivated. But in the last hundred years men have set out purposefully to improve their plants in order to get the taste, form, color, or fragrance they desired.

This is the story of a man, Luther Burbank, who changed plants more than any man had ever done before. He was never satisfied with the berries, fruits and flowers growing around him. He always asked, "What can they become?" "How can I improve them?" He wanted larger, more colorful and sweeter smelling flowers. He wanted tastier, bigger, richer or sweeter fruits. And he achieved these things. Our dinner tables and our gardens have not been the same since he started on his life-long campaign of "training plants to work for man." He became a legend in his lifetime, one of the three most world-famous living Americans. Thomas Edison was known for lighting houses by electricity. Henry Ford's name meant an automobile to millions. Luther Burbank's name stood for the invention of new and improved plants.

The "gardener touched with genius," converted the nursery man's trade into a huge and spectacular enterprise. Millions acclaimed him a wizard and a wonderworker. Some condemned him as a charlatan who took advantage of the public's gullibility. While the debate raged round his head, Burbank quietly cultivated his experimental garden, confident that he was producing "better fruits and fairer flowers."

There once lived an English landscape and sea painter who painted brilliant sunsets. English sunsets have been to many people more colorful and beautiful since Joseph Turner opened their eyes to them. Something similar happened to our fruits and flowers since Burbank. But there is an important difference. Turner made the sunsets *appear* more beautiful by showing colors in them people hadn't observed before. Luther Burbank *made* the fruits more lucious and the flowers more beautiful.

Creating new and better plants
LUTHER BURBANK

Chapter 1

Growing Up in Massachusetts

In the center of Massachusetts is a small town named Lancaster. Stately elms arch over its streets. Surrounding the town are hills and valleys, lovely woods and lakes.

Lancaster is fifteen miles from Concord where the first battles of the Revolutionary War were fought and where, later, two great writers lived—Ralph Waldo Emerson and Henry David Thoreau. Lancaster is also famous as the birthplace and early home of Luther Burbank. He was just a boy when Emerson and Thoreau were famous men.

Luther Burbank was born in 1849. He lived in a big square house just three miles north of the center of town, in a house full of older half-brothers and half-sisters, a younger brother, Alfred, and a still younger sister, Emma.

The house was surrounded by a hundred acres of farmland and woodland, belonging to Luther's father. Samuel Walton Burbank was a successful farmer who also worked a clay pit on his property to make pottery and bricks. The trees in the woodlands were cut for fuel for the brick kiln.

There was lots of work for a young boy to do on the farm. Luther's first job was to take care of a big maltese cat and other household pets—bantam chickens, guinea pigs, and a pair of white rabbits. Later he cut wood, drove the cows to pasture, fed the chickens, and weeded and hoed in the vegetable garden. Once in a while he drove the oxen with a load of bricks to nearby towns.

Luther's father often took the small children of the family to the woods and taught them the names of flowers and trees. He showed them the burrows of the woodchuck, the nests of squirrels and birds. By the time Luther went to school he could take other children to where the biggest blueberries grew. He could show them where to find the best chestnuts and hickory nuts. He knew how to make popguns from elderwood, and whistles from willows. He could make bows and arrows from beech and hazel, and toy canoes from white birch bark.

Luther's mother took care of a beautiful flower garden that surrounded the house. She had daffodils, tulips, peonies and pinks in the spring. As the summer wore on, phlox, petunias, snapdragons, roses and sunflowers came into bloom. She knew how to make things grow, and she taught her son the fundamentals of gardening. He learned to set bulbs in the garden, to plant seeds in cold-frames to give the plants a head start, and to water, cultivate, and fertilize the soil.

The boy spent a great deal of time in the vegetable garden, too, among the peas and beans, the onions, carrots and turnips, the tomatoes and cabbages. There were pumpkins growing among the corn stalks in the field, and he loved to cut his initials with a penknife on the little pumpkins. Then he would watch the *L.B*'s get bigger as the pumpkins grew. One summer a circus parade gave him an idea. That fall the outlines of elephants, lions and other circus attractions on his pumpkins caused much amusement.

Every summer Luther watched his father select seed for the following year's crops. He saw him take seeds from the earliest ripening large tomato, the most perfect ear of corn, the tastiest melon and the biggest pumpkin.

While young Burbank was growing up, great changes were taking place in the United States. Many New Englanders were leaving their homes for the new fields and pastures of the West. The discovery of gold in California in 1848, just the year before Luther was born, added to the westward movement. Many of those who stayed home were leaving the farms and going to work in the new factories that were springing up in eastern cities and towns. A storm was brewing over slavery, and abolitionists were traveling from place to place preaching that the system was evil and had to be abolished.

During this time, a great intellectual battle reached America from England. In 1859 Charles Darwin published the *Origin of Species*. The theory of evolution that Darwin put forth in his book shook people's notions about themselves and the world they lived in. The teaching that each species of animals and plants had not been specially created by God, but had evolved from one form to another through the ages, started a heated argument. New England ministers thundered against Darwin, and their sermons were echoed in every home.

Luther listened eagerly to the discussions that went on around him. Ministers, teachers, lecturers, and scientists were frequent visitors at the Burbank farm. His cousin, Professor Levi Burbank, was head of the department of geology of the Boston Society of Natural History, and on his visits to Lancaster he would take Luther on long nature walks, teach him the names of rocks, trees and flowers, and inspire him to observe things carefully. Once he brought with him the world famous biologist, Professor Louis Agassiz of Harvard University. Agassiz was the leading scientific opponent of Darwin in America.

At the age of fifteen, Luther entered the Lancaster Academy. Every day he had to walk three miles to get there and three miles back. This was a pleasure for him, for he liked walking; he kept his eyes and ears open for the sights and sounds of nature around him. At this time he read Thoreau, who he thought had begun to translate "Nature into our American language."

Luther's cousin inspired him to observe nature.

"His exuberant joy," Burbank remarked years later, "over the mountains and intervales, and valleys and ponds, was communicated to me. I fell in love with my own country, and its various and peculiar charm delight-ed my boy's heart and mind."

Luther showed no outstanding abilities as a student, but he was a constant reader of science books he borrowed from the Lancaster Public Library.

During the summers of these academy—high school —years, the young Burbank was sent to Worcester to learn a trade. He had always shown mechanical ability, and as a child he had experimented with making wind-mills, water wheels, and miniature steam engines. At the Ames Plow Works, during the summer months, he turned a lathe to make plow handles, earning fifty cents a day. He boarded with an uncle who was a foreman in the plant and paid him fifty cents a day for his board. But since Burbank worked only six days a week and there were seven for which he had to pay board, he was always behind fifty cents a week. This struck him as a poor business arrangement, so he persuaded his uncle to pay him by the piece instead of by the day. Then he invented an improvement for the lathe that enabled him to turn out so much more work that his earnings jumped to as high as sixteen dollars a day. The company was pleased with Burbank and his invention. But after finishing the Academy in 1868, he decided to leave the factory. The clouds of dust that rose from the oak be-ing turned into plow handles began to make him ill.

Just at this time, a new world opened to him. In the Lancaster Library he found a book that had been pub-lished in England that same year. Its title was *The Varia-tion of Plants and Animals under Domestication,* written by the man who had shocked the world nine years earlier with his theory of the evolution of species, Charles Darwin. In this book Burbank was introduced to a startling truth stated in simple language. Cross-breeding different varieties leads to new combinations of characters in plants and in animals. Then selective characters can be fixed in new plants. In other words, man can change the qualities of plants to suit his purpose. Burbank resolved immediately to make this his lifework. He had no facilities for accomplishing his aim, but this one ambition dominated his life from that time on.

That December Burbank's father died. His mother decided to give up the big farm and sell the house. She bought a house in Lunenberg, north of Lancaster near the New Hampshire border. Alfred, the younger brother, set out for California where two of his half-brothers had already settled. This left Burbank and Emma at home with their mother, for the other children had long since grown up and left. Burbank, with his share from the sale of his father's farm, was able to buy seventeen acres of land adjoining their new home. He immediately set to work raising vegetables for the market in the neighboring city of Fitchburg, four and a half miles away.

He found himself competing with well-established and experienced market gardeners. But he learned the tricks of his trade quickly. In a season or two he was taking first-rate vegetables to the market. He even developed special methods to get his produce mature and ripe ahead of that of his competitors, so that he was able to get a better price.

One morning in the summer of 1872 he hit upon a discovery that marked a turning-point in his life. Among the leaves of a potato plant, Burbank saw a seed ball. As everyone knew, potatoes are grown from the "eyes" of old potatoes, not from seeds which the plants rarely produce. This New England variety was generally small, of a reddish color, and did not keep well. What would happen if he planted the seeds from this rare seed ball? By the end of the summer, when the ball ripened, he had twenty-three seeds. Some were as small as pin-heads, others larger, but he carefully saved them all through the winter.

As soon as the ground was ready the following spring he planted his potato seeds. Twenty-three potato plants came up and each one was carefully labelled and numbered. When it came time to dig them up he found a few potatoes in each hill. Some were worthless—with pink and red flesh, and one kind had eyes that reached almost to the center of the potatoes. But seven hills had potatoes that looked promising, and those in the hills numbered 15 and 17 looked exceptionally fine. They were large, smooth and white, better than any potatoes he had ever seen.

That September Burbank exhibited at the annual agricultural fair in Fitchburg. His long table was heaped with fruits of exceptional quality, and with bouquets of flowers and jars of jam and jelly his mother provided. But the plates containing his selected potatoes attracted most attention.

An important distributor of seeds, Mr. J. J. Gregory of Marblehead, offered to buy the rights to potato number 15 if, after trial, it lived up to his expectations. Burbank agreed. Mr. Gregory tested the potato himself and was more pleased than he expected to be. It was a superior variety and gave a yield twice that of the potatoes then being grown. He sent for Burbank and offered to buy the new variety outright. The deal was closed for $150, and Mr. Gregory got the exclusive right to distribute the potato in the East. He announced that he would name it the *Burbank* potato. This was the first of Luther Burbank's "plant creations."

In his catalog that year, Mr. Gregory described the merits of the new potato. "In quality it is firm grained, of excellent flavor either boiled or baked, is dry and floury, is fine, is all that can be desired," he wrote. The *Burbank* potato is still grown from coast to coast, in several different strains, and under different names. Few people have heard of the *Russet Burbank*, but everyone knows it under its trade name—the *Idaho Baker*.

After his success with the potato, Burbank decided to pull up stakes and go to California. He was eager to get away from Massachusetts. He had had an unhappy love affair, and most of his friends and relatives were completely opposed to his idea of a career of producing new varieties of plants. He knew that the California climate was just what he needed for his work. There he could grow plants all year round; in New England he could grow plants only during the summer months. He had heard much about the country and its climate from his three brothers. Burbank wanted to strike out on new lines, for he felt he had a mission in life. It was to make plants work for man, to improve all kinds of plants as he had the potato.

Chapter 2

Another Young Man Goes West

Luther Burbank sat looking intently out the window of a day-coach on a westward bound train. It was early fall of 1875 and he was now a handsome young man of twenty-six. On the seat beside him was a big basket of food his mother had prepared for his long trip. Beneath it was a suitcase containing all his belongings. The most precious of these were ten potatoes that Mr. Gregory had allowed him to keep for use on the West Coast. His ticket had cost him all but ten of the $150 he had received for his potato, and his total savings did not amount to more than five hundred dollars.

The trip to California in 1875 was a strange and exciting experience for a young New England farmer. Stage

Traveling across the continent was a fascinating experience.

coaches and wagon trains had given way to the transcontinental railroad only six years before. The trains were crude and slow; it took nine days and nights to get from Worcester to San Francisco. He and his fellow passengers had to change cars nine times, and make an overnight stay in a hotel at Council Bluffs, Iowa. There were long unscheduled stops, too, when axles overheated or the engine broke down.

Burbank slept sitting, or curled up in his seat, and he ate from his lunch basket. The sandwiches ran out by the time he reached Iowa, but he wrote home that he had enough cake to carry him to California and back.

Despite its hardships, the trip had its rewards. The train crossed the Niagara River over the new suspension bridge, and Burbank saw the great falls. He was amazed at the endless fields of corn he saw crossing Iowa. Then came the desert! From Cheyenne, in Wyoming Territory, he wrote a postcard home, telling of jogging over the rails all day without seeing a tree or a bush more than a foot high. But the passengers enjoyed themselves watching the prairie dogs and the antelopes. After four hundred miles of desert he found the rest of the way "beautiful beyond description." "Mountains," he wrote his mother and Emma, "were piled on mountains, snow-clad peaks gilded with sunlight, wild forests, rivers, deep cuts, mammoth trees."

They went down through the famed Donner Pass into the great Sacramento Valley of central California. Gardens appeared with olives, oleander, and fuchias. He saw front yards ornamented with palm trees, century plants and fig trees—products of the semi-tropics he had known only from books. Burbank was thrilled with the first sight of the land in which he was going to make his home.

He enjoyed two days and nights in San Francisco, delighted with the hilly city's "healing, balmy breezes."

While walking along the city streets, he bought a pear from a street fruit stand. It cost five cents, but he had never seen anything like it. A pear so big he couldn't eat it all! What fruit California had!

But San Francisco was not Burbank's destination. He had fixed his mind on Santa Rosa, in Sonoma County, fifty miles to the north of the big city. His younger brother, Alfred, was living there, and two older brothers were not many miles away. But much as he liked his brothers, he had not traveled three thousand miles to be with them. His one consideration was the conditions most suitable for growing plants.

Santa Rosa surpassed his fondest expectations. He found the climate perfect, the air so sweet it was a pleasure to breathe. The sun flooded the valley with a pure, soft light. It was the very end of October, but he found "the birds singing and everything like a beautiful spring day all the time." And the fruits and flowers! Twelve-foot high fuchsias in front yards, great rose *trees* climbing over the houses, bunches of grapes half a yard long, cabbages as big as washtubs.

The uncultivated hillsides were covered with wild flowers, and in all his walks he could find no place which "nature had not made perfectly lovely." He confessed to his mother and sister that he almost had to cry for joy at the beautiful plants and trees he saw. "As far as *Nature* is concerned," he said, "it is the chosen spot of all this earth."

This was all very enjoyable, but Burbank had work and a place to live. Alfred and another man had just built themselves an eight-by-ten-foot shanty, and they invited Luther to move in with them. The night of his arrival the three of them went shopping for bedding and cooking utensils to start housekeeping. Burbank was pleased at how cheaply they could live. Even though it was getting into November, no heat was necessary. Fruit cost almost nothing. They could even go to the vineyards and help themselves to grapes. At the end of the week the three men figured out the cost of housekeeping, and it came to only $1.94 each. They ordered additional supplies; ten pounds of oatmeal, canned salmon, a bag each of sweet potatoes, onions, and apples, and various incidentals. Burbank's savings would last a while at this rate. What did he need? he asked himself. Only a place to sleep, food and clothing! The first two were cheap and easy to come by. And he needed very little clothing.

He spent a month in perfect contentment. It seemed like a whole lifetime. It was as if he had crawled out of a dungeon into morning sunshine. He worked a few days as a carpenter on a hotel being built in Santa Rosa, but spent the rest of the time visiting his older brothers in near-by towns and in tramping the countryside collecting plants. On one long walk he found a wild spot of about an acre with enough new and curious plants "to set a botanist mad." Having met an old surveyor who knew nearly

[27]

all the plants of the area, he took him his new finds to identify. Burbank found that his botany book listed only a few California plants, and that some of his discoveries had *never even been named.*

After the first month Burbank grew impatient. He had decided to take only short jobs, because he wanted either to rent or buy land and start a nursery in which he could work evenings. But now the rains came, and they put an end to all kinds of building work. He was going "dead broke."

One morning in December he decided to walk the nineteen miles to Petaluma to look for work. At seven-thirty he started out through terrible mud. He stopped at several farmhouses asking for the opportunity to work for a meal and wait 'til the rains stopped. He was turned down everywhere. "I won't make my fortune that way," he told himself, as he trudged along through rain and mud. All day he had nothing to eat but a slice of bread. It was six o'clock in the evening when he reached Petaluma.

The next morning he applied for work at the Petaluma Greenhouses and Nurseries. Mr. Pepper, owner of the establishment that included large greenhouses, two great nurseries, a fruit farm and a ranch, first told him there was no work. "I have too much help already," he said. But when Luther Burbank told him of his experience, Mr. Pepper agreed to take him on. Burbank could live in a little room over one of the greenhouses and board with the family. Besides room and board, he would receive $30 a month in wages. He was delighted with the offer and agreed to start work Monday. He then walked back to Santa Rosa for his belongings.

The new job would carry him over the rainy season when no houses were being built. Then, when spring came, he intended to quit the job, get some land for himself and work as a carpenter for $3.50 to $4.00 a day. Such a job would keep him from eating into his small capital and enable him to save a hundred dollars or so in the bargain. Meanwhile, his chief asset, the ten potatoes he had brought from Massachusetts, were in the ground at his brother George's place. Next year he would plant all the new ones again, and by the end of 1877 he would have a new product to offer California seedsmen.

On Sunday, December 5, Burbank wrote hopefully to his mother and sister. He told them of his job and his plans, but especially of his surroundings.

"Today is the most lovely one," he wrote. "The thermometer is 65° in the shade. I sit here writing with two open windows and a wide-open door. The warm pleasant sunshine pouring in on the floor, birds singing, trees green and fresh, the ground carpeted with long green grass, and castor-oil plants in full bloom around the shanty. The roses have taken a new start since the rain, and instead of having a few stray buds as they do in June, they are in great *clusters*, 20-60 in a cluster, like grapes."

The land and the climate were beautiful, but Burbank's hardships were just beginning. He worked in Mr. Pepper's greenhouses and nurseries throughout his first winter in California. By spring he was exhausted from working in the damp soil by day and spending his nights in a steamy room above the greenhouse. He caught a fever, quit the job, and returned ill to Santa Rosa. When he recovered he rented several acres of land. Working at carpenter jobs during the day, he used his evenings to start raising fruits and vegetables.

Those first years were ones of dreadfully hard work and bitter struggle. In 1877 his mother and sister Emma came to California. His mother bought a house in Santa Rosa where the three of them lived. By the end of that year, Burbank had potatoes to sell, not to eat but to plant. He found them not easy to market, however, because they were so different from those to which people were accustomed. He decided that for the time being he had better raise such fruits and vegetables as would be immediately acceptable to the people of the vicinity.

The total sales from his nursery in 1877 amounted to only $15.20. The next year they increased to $84 and the third year to $353.28. He derived a little income, too, from collecting seeds of California plants for several United States and European seed firms.

By the end of 1880, five years after pulling up stakes

and moving to California, Luther Burbank had a growing nursery business, but he was still far from his consuming ambition. He had not come to California to be a practical nurseryman, merely selling young plants that anyone could raise. He wanted to create new ones. When and how, he constantly asked himself, would he have the opportunity to devote his time and labor to new plant creations?

Chapter 3

The Turning Point: His First Big Order

One March afternoon in 1881, Luther Burbank was walking home from a carpentering job, worrying over his problems. His thirty-second birthday was approaching and he was uncomfortably aware that he was late getting started on his life's work.

When he reached home he found Mr. Warren Dutton waiting for him. Dutton was a wealthy merchant and banker of Petaluma who had bought some trees from Burbank the year before. When they had greeted each other and were seated, Dutton offered Burbank an amazing opportunity. Dutton owned two hundred acres of land outside of Petaluma on which he wanted to plant plums that would make good prunes. It would take twenty thousand trees, he figured, to use the land profitably. Several nurserymen he had approached had turned him down. Could Burbank provide the trees?

Burbank suppressed his excitement at the size of the order. This was nursery business on a scale he had never heard of before. He could do it, he thought, if he put every thing else aside. He accepted the proposition and asked when the trees would be wanted.

That was the hitch! Dutton was in a hurry. He was determined to get the orchard going at the earliest possible moment. The trees must be ready to set out that fall.

Now Burbank knew why the others had turned him down. Growing 20,000 plum trees in one season—that was something unheard of. No nurseries anywhere in the world carried such stock, and plum trees could not be grown from seed in one year. "Only in such a climate as California's," he told himself, "could it even be thought of." He concealed his hesitations and doubts while he replied that he would have to think it over. It was a rule of his, he told Dutton, never to sign papers or obligate himself to anything important until he could sleep on it and examine it again the next day.

Dutton agreed to wait for Burbank's decision. Before leaving he told Burbank that he knew it would require considerable outlay and that he was prepared to advance whatever financial aid would be required. But he made it clear that the orchard had to be planted with twenty thousand plum trees before the year was out.

Burbank was excited. Here was the challenge he had been waiting for. All the time Dutton was talking, Burbank thought, "This is just what I need. One such order carried through successfully and I can give up my carpentering altogether and devote full time to the nursery business." Once that was running well, he could begin to work on his life ambition—the development of new and improved varieties of plants.

He well knew that prune trees wouldn't spout from seeds fast enough. But a thought struck him; almonds would. They sprout almost at once, and are closely related to the plum. If he could get them started in good time he could then graft plum buds on them. He knew he could get plenty of these by June and July from the French plums in his own and neighboring nurseries. Perhaps he could have them ready in the fall at that!

At dinner that evening with Emma and his mother, the order for the twenty thousand plum trees was the only subject of conversation. He would have to rent five acres in addition to the two he had already rented. Could he get the almonds immediately? Would he be able to hire enough men to get the whole project underway?

Fortunately, the house he was working on was about finished. There would be no more carpentering for him this year, and if this project worked out he could give up carpentering altogether.

The evening hours were spent calculating the land, materials, and labor required for the job. He tried to figure the costs and to plan the organization of the many steps required. It was an enormous enterprise, but it could be done, he concluded, and he would do it.

In bed that night Burbank vowed that he was not going to be content with making those plum trees this year and then doing the same kind of thing the rest of his life. This would help him only to get started. In the years ahead he was going to make new and better plums; larger, sweeter and meatier ones; better plums, too, for prunes. He thought of prunes with more sugar, smaller pits, better flavor, more body, better skins for drying, and with more plums on every tree every year.

California was a fabulous state, he thought, as his mind swam with visions of endless orchards of plum trees, plums of every kind, plums for every purpose. They could be worth more than all the gold in California now that people were discovering the wealth in the prune as an article of commerce to ship east. The new transcontinental railroad made this possible. And there weren't enough prunes being grown and dried to satisfy the demand.

At daybreak, as usual, Burbank was up. He reviewed the whole project from every angle. He could find no flaws, no objections. After breakfast he drove to Petaluma and as calmly as possible informed Dutton that he would accept the proposition. He told him of the almonds

[36]

that sprouted almost at once and that they made a most satisfactory stock, or foster-parent, for plums. Dutton agreed to pay at once for the almonds. Other details were worked out, and the deal was concluded.

There was great excitement in the Burbank household. Much planning had to be done: the almonds purchased, the best possible land rented, help hired to prepare the sprouting beds and the ground into which the young sprouts would be set. Burbank had to figure exactly where he would get twenty thousand plum buds he would need by June and July, and the skilled grafters he would require to set them on the almond stock.

During the next few days he went enthusiastically about his many tasks. They required more than his knowledge as a nurseryman. Never before in his life had he organized such a big project, requiring so much help and so many separate tasks in different stages. He succeeded in buying enough almonds of the desired quality. He found five acres of good land near the two he already had for his nursery. He arranged to hire a number of men to help prepare the sprouting bed and to plant the almonds when they started sprouting.

He laid the almonds out on a specially prepared bed of coarse sand. Then he put burlap over them and covered that with a layer of about an inch of sand. Once he had the almonds in their "bed" the next step was to prepare the five acres for planting. The land was plowed and neat nursery rows, four feet apart, were laid out.

Luther examined his almonds daily, lifting up the burlap. At last, on the twelfth day some of them had tiny sprouts showing. Immediately the work of planting commenced. Each sprouted almond was carefully picked out and placed in trays to be carried to the newly prepared land. Here, in the rows already prepared, the sprouts were planted about four inches apart. It was hard and tedious work. Hundreds were planted, but there were still thousands upon thousands to come.

Each morning the cloth and sand covering was removed and the almonds that had sprouted taken to the orchard and planted. By the time the last ones had been set out, the earliest plantings were already showing above the ground. Now there was nothing to do but wait for them all to grow to the right size. Nothing, that is, but cultivate the soil, and keep it free from weeds and in the best possible condition for the tender young shoots to flourish.

The first stage of the job had been accomplished and Burbank watched carefully over his nursery of twenty thousand young trees. Under the strong California sun the green seedlings were getting taller every day.

All had gone well so far, Burbank thought, as he counted up the operations that had been performed. Laying the almonds out on the sprouting bed, one; taking them up again, two; planting them in the soil, three. That made sixty thousand distinct operations. But the job had just begun, for all he had was an orchard of baby almond trees. In a few months they would all have to be transformed into plum trees. This would take at least five different steps for each tree: a staggering figure of a hundred thousand more operations.

Everything now depended on the almonds being tall and strong enough for grafting when the new buds on the plum trees would be ready. It was near the end of June when the buds reached the right stage. Luther hired a large force of men to cut off the small buds and graft them on the almond stems. Each almond stem had to be cut into, the bud carefully placed on the cut, tied to the stem and sealed with wax. This task took the rest of June and all of July and August.

He allowed the buds about ten days to become thoroughly joined to the almond stems and then another operation had to begin. This consisted of breaking over the tops of the young almond trees. He knew that if the tops were cut off altogether the plants would most certainly die. He had the men take great care to see that the tops were broken down but still left alive.

One day soon after, thousands of young plum buds began to burst forth. That was the signal for the beginning of still another operation. They must tie each of the young growing buds to the almond stem in order to get a good straight tree.

Finally, when the stems from the plum buds had

grown a foot high the old almond tops were cut off. Now the transformation was complete. The young plum buds had taken over. In place of a great orchard of almond seedlings there was now an orchard of plum trees growing from the original almond stock.

It was on the first day of December that Luther Burbank informed Dutton that his trees were ready for delivery. He apologized for being five hundred trees short. His rough count came to nineteen-thousand-five hundred, and Dutton would have to wait till next year for the remainder. Dutton was not worried about the exact number after every other nurseryman had told him that the job was impossible. As they shook hands he exclaimed, "Mr. Burbank, you're a wizard."

Burbank's reputation was made. Talk of his feat spread through Sonoma County and into neighboring counties. He began to be known widely as "The Wizard of Santa Rosa," just as Thomas Edison on the other side of the country was known as "The Wizard of Menlo Park." One had a nursery and the other a laboratory, and the products of both were to become known around the world in the decades to come.

Actually, Burbank had done nothing scientifically new in producing the plum orchard in one year. Similar methods has been used in some southern states for the propagation of peaches. The process was known as June budding. But what Burbank did was new to California, and had been performed on a larger scale than had ever been attempted before. The feat took daring and imagination. This achievement was more like those that kept Henry Ford a step ahead of his competitors than it was like Edison's inventions.

The Dutton order came at the right moment. Prune growing was proving profitable. The eastern market was an insatiable market for fruit, but there were big risks in shipping fresh fruits because there was no railroad refrigeration. Sun-dried prunes, however, could be sent great distances without injury. Prunes were a sure-fire crop, and prune orchards were rapidly increasing in California's great Central Valley. Planters began to line up at Burbank's nursery to give him their orders.

His nursery business expanded rapidly. He decided he would be able to make a living from it, while gradually devoting more and more of his time and resources to experimenting with plants in the search for new and improved varieties. It was now clear to him just what he would do the rest of his life. He would be a nurseryman's nurseryman. He would sell not twenty thousand plum trees to a Mr. Dutton, but one tree bearing a new and better plum. His customers would be the nurseries rather than the Dutton's who were planting orchards. He would develop and sell an improved tree and the right to reproduce it. That was exactly what he had done with the potato back home.

Chapter *4*

A New Theory and New Methods

Burbank's nursery business was growing, but his dreams centered on plant development. Ever since reading Darwin's *Animals and Plants under Domestication* back in Massachusetts, his head had been full of questions concerning the origin of new varieties. He had produced a new and better potato, but that was largely an accident. The use of the potato seed-ball could not serve as a model for the improvement of other plants.

Burbank deplored the texts he read. They were enough, he thought, to drive young people away from plants instead of making them exciting. Existing textbooks on botany gave no clues to plant breeders. The botanists seemed to think they knew all about a plant if they

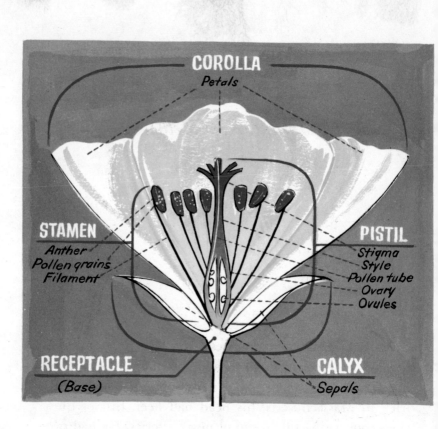

PARTS OF A FLOWER

could pigeon-hole a dead specimen and distinguish it from all other plants. For him, the wonderful thing was the living plant. More wonderful, still, was the fact that no two plants even of the same species were ever exactly alike.

Burbank and the botanists of the time knew nothing yet about the laws of heredity and exactly how characters are transmitted from parent to offspring. But everybody knew that the flower had parts that carried the heredity of the plant.

In the center of every flower are the stamens and pistils. Each stamen has an anther—a little bag of *pollen grains,* at the top. At the bottom of the pistil is the ovary containing *ovules* or the seeds-to-be. Inside the pollen grains and the ovules, Burbank knew, were "specks of protoplasm" that contained the heredity of the plant. (We now call these *genes.*)

When the anthers mature, the pollen grains burst out. At the top of the pistil is a sticky surface called the stigma. When pollen grains land on this surface they start to grow down to the bottom of the pistil where the ovules lie. Now the contents of the pollen grain join with, or *fertilize,* the contents of the ovule or ovules (there may be only one or hundreds of ovules). The ovule then ripens and turns into a seed.

In some flowers the anthers burst open just as the stigma of the same flower is ready to receive the pollen grains. In this case, the flower is *self-pollinated.* But in many flowers the stamens and pistils ripen at different times. The anthers shed pollen before the stigma is ripe. Or the stigma may have already ripened and received pollen from other flowers before the anthers of its own flower start to shed their pollen. Because of this, pollination in such flowers only takes place by *cross-pollination.* The pollen must be brought from other flowers of the same kind by wind, insects, or birds.

Self-pollinated flowers produce seeds that carry heredity identical to that of the parent plant. Such plants tend to remain the same indefinitely. But when flowers are cross-pollinated, the pollen grains bring one set of heredity characteristics and the ovules another set. This mixes the heredity in the new plant and brings about changes, or variations. Such things go on all the time in nature. But man, by the simple process of transferring the pollen of one flower to the pistil of another flower of the same species, can make his own variations.

"I do not know anything in the work of the plant developer," Burbank explained, "that offers him more pleasure and satisfaction than this process. Fellow to the bee, the hummingbird, the ant and the butterfly, he goes from blossom to blossom. . . . Like a painter choosing the colors for his palette, I choose the qualities that I desire to combine. . . ."

Burbank was helped immensely in his ideas for changing plants by another book of Darwin's, *Cross and Self-Fertilization in the Vegetable Kingdom*. Burbank got a copy of this not long after it was published in 1877. One sentence in the opening chapter, he reported later, "opened the door of my mind and took possession of my fancy." Darwin, discussing how plants had developed methods to insure cross-pollination, had written:

As plants are adapted by such diversified and effective means for cross-fertilization, it might have been inferred from this fact alone that they derived some great advantage from the process; and it is the object of the present work to show the nature and importance of the benefits thus derived.

This sentence gave Burbank the second great inspiration for his lifework.

"Advantages and benefits!" he exclaimed. "Darwin was writing of the plants themselves—I was thinking of mankind. If Nature had developed an incredible system by which plants could re-create and diversify and improve themselves *for their own benefit* and advantage, why should not Nature be induced to employ that same system *for the benefit and advantage of man?* It was my starting point—and it was Darwin again!"

What nature did over innumerable generations in changing plant-forms, man could do artificially in a relatively few years. Man could do this by selecting the individuals that had the qualities he wanted to strengthen and develop, and by suppressing all others.

Burbank approached the task of improving plants with four general ideas in mind. Can unused wild plants be developed into something useful or beautiful? Can the quality and beauty of already used plants be improved? Can useful plants be extended to greater ranges of climate and soil conditions? And finally, can a given plant produce a larger yield or serve man by growing faster?

Once Burbank had an idea of the direction in which he wanted a given plant to go, he searched at home and through collectors all over the world for the best materials to work with. One of the collectors he was particularly indebted to was Señor José D. Husbands of Chile, who scaled mountain peaks, waded rivers, visited islands, and traveled through wild arid deserts to collect new species for Burbank. Amateur collectors from scattered points of the globe sent him seeds of strange or unusual plants. Travelers visiting isolated areas carried back little envelopes of seeds they later mailed to Burbank. The volunteers helping his work numbered thousands.

The essence of Burbank's method was to bring together through cross-pollination many different plant strains from widely separated parts of the world. By cross-pollination he combined the various hereditary factors they contained.

The next step was selection. After the seeds from his special crosses had grown, the plants were examined closely for the qualities Burbank wanted. Burbank used his eyes, his nose, and his mouth as he walked through his gardens, smelling, tasting, and noting differences in color, shape, and form. In the case of fruits and vegetables he took the products right into the kitchen and the whole family became involved in cooking or preserving, or making jelly, soup, or stew. Selection here became "a matter for palate and nose, or even for the stomach and the digestive processes," as well as one of eye and touch and aesthetic measurement.

The plants he thought promising were *selected*. All others were destroyed. Usually he lit big bonfires to burn plants that were inspected and found wanting. "To burn 65,000 hybrid blackberries in one pile, as I once did after saving perhaps half a dozen individual vines seems like wilful extravagance to the casual observer, but it is an unavoidable incident in the search for perfect fruits," Burbank wrote.

Nature, according to Darwin, selected by the law of the survival of the fittest. In successive generations, those individuals less fitted to cope with their environment died out, while the more fit survived. This process of natural selection was slow; it might take thousands of years to produce a noticeable change in a species. Besides, the plants that won out might or might not be more beautiful or more useful to man. But Burbank could select artificially the qualities he especially wanted in his plants. He also could speed up nature's work. As he once said, he took nature's laws and added to them his own mind "that knew exactly what it wanted and was in a hurry to get it."

During the same years when Burbank was forming his theory and aims, a Russian named Ivan Michurin was embarking on the same path. He, too, read Darwin, and like Burbank was not satisfied to wait for better varieties to occur naturally by chance and then to propagate from these to obtain an improved variety. His slogan was: "We cannot wait for favors from Nature: we must wrest them from her." Darwin thus inspired a new type of scientific horticulture, of plant improvement, on almost opposite sides of the earth. The most interesting thing about this application of Darwin's theories to horticulture is that Darwin himself derived his idea of natural selection from the artificial selection that had long been practiced by animals and plant breeders. But once Darwin's theories were formulated, it became possible for horticulturists to do systematically and scientifically what they had done before Darwin by mere rule of thumb, based solely on what worked.

Burbank was in a hurry to produce new and better plants in his own lifetime, and he used mass production methods to make this possible. Filling the order for twenty thousand prune trees had shown him the possibility of doing experimental work on a gigantic scale. He took a lesson from the rapidly expanding industries in the United States. He was not only going to "speed up production," but was going to "build up and maintain quantity production." The chance of finding good varieties, he knew, increased with the number of plants he examined. He planted thousands of seedlings where others before him had dealt in hundreds. In developing the Shasta Daisy he tested half a million young plants. His work with plums involved seven and a half million plum plants. This method could produce results in a few years that would take thousands of years if nature were left to follow its own course.

Burbank once told a friend of the kind of pressure he was under, compared to Nature's unconcern. "She wasn't under contract," he said, "and no one was writing her indignant letters beginning, 'In the matter of the shipment of pine trees ordered from you five hundred years ago for our temperate climate, beg to advise you that same has not yet arrived.'" Nature had all the time there was and all the raw materials needed. She could be wasteful and extravagant and leisurely. But Burbank was planning to produce new varieties in his own lifetime. He thought of himself as a plant architect who would produce a new plant as an architect designs a new building. He was going to make plants to order. Just as the architect shapes raw materials provided by nature to serve human purpose, Burbank was going to use the raw materials from nature—wild seeds, cuttings from native and foreign plants—domesticate them as one tames wild animals, and then rearrange or combine them to secure the various traits desired.

There were short-cut methods available to Burbank for some plants. Lilies, for example, reproduce from bulbs and once he obtained a good variety, it was easy to make more of exactly the same kind of plant. A lily bulb can be taken apart scale by scale, and each scale planted in the ground will grow into a tiny new bulb that can grow into a garden-size bulb in two or three seasons. Besides, most bulbs naturally divide underground, so that a whole clump of new bulbs can often be found around the original one. This type of reproduction is called *asexual* because it does not involve the reproductive organs—the stamens and pistils.

Another type of asexual reproduction Burbank depended on was the use of cuttings. Cuttings are pieces of a stem or branch that root when put into water or soil. After roots form, the cutting becomes a plant. Roses, willows and many other plants root in this easy way.

But the branches of some trees do not root easily. With such trees Burbank used grafting. Once he obtained a good variety of plum, for example, he could graft a branch or bud of the new type onto another tree with a strong root system. In this way, a whole new tree would grow out, in a short time, from a single branch or bud. This was the method he used to produce the twenty thousand plum trees for his first big order. The two parts had to be tied together tightly so that the growing layers (cambium) just under the bark were in contact. This insured the two parts growing together, and then the new branch could grow out into a brand new top on an old tree bottom.

Burbank grafted his hybrid plums by the hundreds onto the same old tree, and had hundreds of such trees, each covered with an astonishing variety of fruit. When visitors pointed to any such tree and asked, "What kind of tree is that, Mr. Burbank," he sometimes replied, "Why, it is hardly fair to speak of that as a tree; that is a concentrated plum orchard." He had one cherry tree colony that he loved to compare to New York's celebrated Four Hundred, for he had four hundred pedigreed cherries growing on one single tree.

And so by seeking far and wide for interesting varieties to cross, by planting thousands upon thousands of seeds and selecting the few best from each such lot, by using grafting on a huge scale, Burbank set the stage for his fabulous reputation to come.

Chapter 5

"New Creations"

It took Burbank twelve years to complete the transition from nurseryman to full-time plant breeder. His years of privation were over, but the years when he was beginning his real life's work were years of arduous labor.

His nursery business grew and prospered. He bought four new acres of land across the street from the home he shared with his mother, but they were soon insufficient for all the work he wanted to do. Near the end of 1885 he received a second big consignment of seeds and seedlings he had ordered from Japan, including a large variety of plums. Immediately, he bought an eighteen-acre farm at Sebastopol, seven miles from Santa Rosa, where these new plants could be placed and nurtured. Years later he told how, with this purchase, his "project of devoting a lifetime to the work of plant experimentation was fairly and finally inaugurated." He needed this additional land not for a practical nursery to raise trees to sell, but as an experimental garden for the creation of new varieties on a large scale.

Thus, at the age of thirty-six, Burbank was beginning the new phase of the life work he had dreamed of ever since setting out for California. But there were still a number of hurdles to get over. He was only one man, but he was planning to do work that would ordinarily only be undertaken by an institution with a private endowment or government funds. It would take years before he could have significant new varieties to offer, and even then buyers would not turn up instantly and spontaneously.

The time Burbank had to continue to spend in the nursery business in order to make a living was time taken away from plant development. As he expressed it, he either had to fish or cut bait; he had to be a plant breeder or a commercial nurseryman. He couldn't be both at once.

He realized he would need income from the nursery business for a few more years, even though the die was cast with the plantings and experiments at Sebastopol. So just as he had been a shrewd truck-farmer back in New England, he became a shrewd businessman during this transitional period. In 1887 he published his first real nursery catalog. What distinguished it from those of other nurserymen was that there were more novelties, which were announced as Japanese imports, not previously available in America. Business boomed, allowing him to devote more time and money to developing new plant varieties.

Each year after this, Burbank modestly announced new varieties, ranging from plums to gladioli. But more and more he turned from retailing to the cash sale of his entire stock of a new product. In this way he was steadily changing his customers from individuals to big established nursery firms. Their names, familiar to every gardener include Vaughan, Dreer, Stark Brothers and W. Atles Burpee. Companies as far away as Australia and South Africa became his customers. Working entirely alone, with only hired assistants for routine and manual jobs, he was able to offer something that the biggest and oldest nursery firms in this country and elsewhere were eager to buy. He was becoming established.

In 1892 he mailed out a leaflet complaining that in the East of the United States, planters would not accept something new unless it was first sold in Europe. "For many years," he added, "Eastern seedsmen, florists and nurserymen have been selling as novelties, trees, plants and seeds which originated on my own Experimental Grounds at Santa Rosa." He boasted, in the leaflet, of his labors as well as of the tens of thousands of dollars he had spent on hybridizing plants during the previous twenty-five years. He was growing six hundred thousand hybrid berry plants and more than half a million hybrid lilies which "are producing profound surprise and admiration." In a year or more, he announced, he would introduce two new quinces which will mark "the greatest advance ever made in improving this fruit."

Burbank was growing a bit cocky. He was an ambitious man, forty-three years of age, driven by an extraordinarily exciting idea. He had worked inecessantly from dawn till after dusk almost every day for years. He had staked his future and his fortune on a dream. It took courage and tremendous self-confidence to move into this new path, but Burbank had assessed clearly all the possible advantages and difficulties. He was getting set for a big plunge.

In June, 1893, when Grover Cleveland was in the White House and Victoria was still Queen of England, Burbank launched his "bombshell" as he himself called it. In all history, nothing had ever been seen like Burbank's illustrated catalog, entitled "New Creations in Fruits and Flowers." Under the title was a picture of various luscious fruits, and the advice: "Keep·this Catalog for Reference. You will need it when these Fruits and Flowers become standards of excellence."

This fifty-two page announcement carried pictures and descriptions of nearly a hundred absolutely new plants, flowers, berries, and even trees. The first item listed was a hybrid walnut, named the "Paradox," then came four new quinces, ten new plums, a number of berries, flowers ranging from gladioli to poppies. The booklet ended with an offering of an assortment of improved varieties of vegetables.

Inside the cover-page Burbank explained that the plants listed in his booklet were "new creations, lately produced by scientific combination of Nature's forces, guided by long, carefully conducted, and very expensive biological study." And he concluded this introduction with the prophecy:

> *We are now standing just at the gateway of scientific horticulture, only having taken a few steps in the measureless fields which will stretch out as we advance into the golden sunshine of a more complete knowledge of the forces which are to unfold all the graceful forms of garden beauty, and wealth of fruit and flowers, for the comfort and happiness of Earth's teeming millions.*

Burbank had only a few hundred copies of his unique catalog printed. He mailed them out to dealers. Almost immediately, requests for more catalogs began to come in thick and fast. Colleges, experimental stations, libraries, students, and scientific societies requested copies. More and more were printed and mailed out, and a year later, when he was publishing a "New Creations" for 1894, requests for the original catalog were still arriving. It was even being translated into other languages.

The nurserymen and other dealers responded as Burbank had hoped. He knew that among many of them he already had a reputation, and they would take his claims seriously. He knew, too, that others would accept him in part, but would feel he was exaggerating. And he well understood that large numbers of them would be skeptics and scoffers. For the benefit of the last group he stated in the catalog that he would not engage in long explanations by mail. If anyone did not want to buy outright, on the strength of Burbank's name and reputation, he could come to Santa Rosa and see for himself. Skeptics came, and they bought. One Eastern nurseryman journeyed the three thousand miles to California to see for himself. Getting off the train at Santa Rosa he happened to meet an old man who said he had worked for Burbank for years. He asked the old fellow about Burbank. The answer was something like this "He used to have a big nursery, and he did well at it. But he sold out, and now he raises acres and acres of all sorts of stuff, waters it and cultivates it through the spring and then, when summer comes, he has most of it pulled out and burned. Burned! Did you ever hear of such foolishness? Now he talks about selling the trash he has left, but I wouldn't give him fifty dollars for the whole kit and boodle. That's Burbank!"

The nurseryman told Burbank the story as he went up and down the gardens examining the "New Creations." He selected seven of the hundred and paid $6,000 in cash for them. Before the year was up, Burbank had sold most of the plants and trees he had offered.

The "New Creations" bulletins appeared annually beginning in 1893, and by 1901, on the basis of the first

Colossal bonfires were a yearly event at Burbank's gardens.

eight catalogs, Burbank had sold no less than seven hundred new varieties of flowers, trees, shrubs, vines and grains. His dream of becoming a nurseryman's nurseryman, of marketing a new plum tree, rather than selling orchards of standard trees, had succeeded beyond his wildest dreams. In those eight years, Burbank, working alone, produced and marketed more new varieties than were patented under the 1930 plant patent law in any equal period of time.

Unfortunately, Burbank's first catalog of "New Creations" stirred up a controversy he had not expected. Although he had chosen the phrase carefully, and believed that he could defend himself against any accusations that his offerings were neither *new* nor *creations,* he had completely failed to foresee how some orthodox religious people might react. To some of them, only God can create a new thing. They thought that Burbank, who liked to picture himself as a "partner of nature," was setting himself up as a partner of God. This was blasphemy, and a storm arose over the seemingly innocent title of his plant catalog. One clergyman invited him to listen to a sermon on his work. Burbank attended the service and heard himself denounced "as a man who was working in direct opposition to the will of God, in thus creating new forms of life which never should have been created, or if created, only by God himself."

While dealers bought Burbank's "New Creations," and many religious leaders denounced him, to the general public his catalog presented the most concrete demonstration of evolution they had yet seen. Here were what appeared to be new *species* of plants, and they were of recent and perfectly known origin. As Burbank himself had said of them, "They have been developed under the hand of the experimenter" through methods similar to those employed by *"natural selection* on plants in the state of nature."

Burbank was greatly pleased to be able to exhibit what he had accomplished on the basis of Darwin's theories, and to help the public to understand better what Darwin meant. One of his accomplishments, for example, was the "Primus Berry." It was a new berry brought into being by a cross between a raspberry and a blackberry. One of the parents was a native of California, the other of Siberia. They were so different in appearance that they would be classified as different species. Yet they were crossed and produced fertile offspring that were different from each of the parents. Here was concrete evidence of the origin of a new species.

Burbank had every reason to be pleased with his first catalog. It won him a world-wide reputation. It brought him to the attention of all of the larger horticultural firms in the world. He had proven that his chosen field of work could be pursued successfully. And he had helped to show the truth of Darwin's evolutionary theory.

Chapter 6

Improving the Plum

S ome of my most valuable work has been with the plum," Burbank told his biographer when he was seventy-five years old. "When I began," he continued, "the plum was small, usually acid, generally unfit for shipping, often with a large stone, and sold in a limited number of varieties."

Even more than with most other fruits and flowers, Burbank knew from the beginning exactly what he wanted the plum to be. His first consideration was that it could be shipped without spoiling or losing its flavor. California provided ideal conditions for growing plums but they would be of little value unless they could be delivered and sold throughout most of the United States.

They would have to be large, beautiful and delicious too. Some varieties would have to dry so well that they could be shipped and used as prunes. There was also a need, he thought, for a good canning plum with a small pit or none at all. "My designs were pretty carefully worked out," he said.

As with all his more important ventures in changing plants and inventing new varieties, Burbank tried to trace the plum back to its origins. He knew that there were wild plum trees scattered all over the United States. But the tree seemed to have originated in ancient Mesopotamia, to which scientists then traced many of our plants, animals, and possibly man himself. It was a hardy tree that could adapt itself to widely differing climates and soils. Ancient tribes cultivated it, and birds and animals spread its seeds or pits. Burbank found that it would grow almost anyplace where deciduous (non-evergreen) trees could live.

Nature worked in its own way over countless thousands of years to produce the wild plum. Then man, in a relatively few centuries, made the plum into an edible fairly sweet and juicy fruit. Now Burbank was going to transform the fruit still further, to make it a commercially marketable item. The era of modern packing methods and long distance transportation had arrived, and to make use of these advances, the fruit of trees had to ripen at the same time so they could be picked in one swoop.

They had to be good for canning, drying, and shipping fresh without spoiling or losing their flavor. Burbank looked upon orchard trees as machines that had to produce the proper quality of fruit regularly.

"Did it ever occur to you," Burbank once asked a visitor, "that the building of railroads and the erection of drying plants and canneries marked a new era in the history of plants?"

Early in the 1880's, when Burbank was trying to make a success of his nursery business in order to devote himself to plant experiments, he began to size up the plum as a fruit California could produce and that the rest of the country would buy. Most of the plums then being planted were of a variety that had been imported from France. But just at that time he came across the description an American sailor had written of a blood-red Japanese plum found in the province of Satsuma. It fairly made Burbank's mouth water, and he decided at once to import that plum and others like it from Japan. He sent for a dozen different varieties of Japanese plums.

With these as a foundation, he started his experiments. Within four years he found that two of the Japanese plums had done so well in the California soil and climate that they were already better than their Japanese relatives. He marketed these, and the fruit specialist of the Department of Agriculture at Washington named one the "Burbank" and the other the "Satsuma."

These improved plums were not new inventions, but only the products of what Burbank called "the college course" he gave in the school he ran for plants.

After his success with the Japanese varieties, he began to work on plums in earnest. He went among his orchard of marked trees with notes in his pocket of their performances—the quality of fruit each produced with respect to size, shape, bearing quality, flavor, color, size of pit, and texture. His task with the plum was complicated by the fact that he had several different goals that involved different standards. One set of qualities would make the ideal home-garden plum to be eaten on the spot; another set of qualities would be desirable for the plum that was to be shipped fresh; a third set would make the best plum for canning; a fourth for drying and shipping as prunes.

As he walked among his trees he would find one that was weak and spindly, but bearing a delicious plum. Perhaps another tree was sturdy but bore small, sour fruit. He would fertilize the first with the pollen of the second. He might chance upon a handsome plum that had no flavor. He would cross this with the blossoms of a tree that bore poor-looking but rich, tasty plums. He performed thousands of experiments.

Then came the excitement of watching the fruit form and ripen. More than once, Burbank made himself ill by sampling too many plums as he went from tree to tree or picked different varieties of plums grafted on the same tree. Tasting fruit was, after all, the only way the most important quality of all could be judged, for he never put any other quality of fruits or vegetables or berries above their flavor.

Second only to taste was appearance. Fruits and berries, rhubard and asparagus, walnuts and ears of corn should be good-looking, Burbank believed, as well as tasty. But of plums, especially, he had to ask much more than tastiness and good-looks. All the plums in an orchard had to ripen at the same time for successful commercial use. They must not fall from the tree before they reach the proper ripeness. They must even be easy to pick, and keep well without spoiling. They must dry and cook well.

Burbank was breeding plums not for one standard but a dozen or more that were sometimes in contradiction with one another. The result was that it took years of the hardest work to get plums that measured up to his requirements.

After some 25,000 separate experiments, Burbank got twenty varieties of plums that he considered good. Of these, about a dozen became widely used. A few were so good that within a decade or two of his first prune offerings the United States changed from a prune importing country to an exporting one. The California crop had increased from sixty-four million to two hundred million pounds a year. Whole towns and counties in California were built up on Burbank's plums and grafts were exported and cultivated as far away as South Africa, Borneo and Australia. By the year 1914, his plums made up one-third of the total export from California.

Burbank recognized that the methods he used in developing the plum fell short of the precision that a purely scientific investigation would have required. He was delighted, therefore, one day when a visitor told him the story of a general who couldn't build a bridge his army needed to cross a stream until he had all the plans, specifications and blueprints. While the general was waiting for these, a young solider got the bridge built and suggested the army march across it. Then, he said, they could make the drawings for the bridge at their leisure.

The visitor explained, "You went ahead and produced the fruit, while a more cautious experimenter would have been occupied in designing hybridizing methods, testing the inheritance of single characteristics, and wouldn't have been ready to start actual construction of new plums by the time you finished."

One of the more weird varieties of plum resulting from Burbank's experiments was a plum he called "Combination." From its seed one could get plums of at least twenty different well-known varieties. It had a pedigree, sure enough, but was the product of multitudes of crossings during more than thirty years, and involving tens of thousands of seedlings. Burbank readily admitted the only thing he knew about it was the original parents he first used. Estimating that something like seven and a half million seedling plums had passed under his hand and eye, he could scarcely be expected to have recorded every combination that had occurred in his experimental gardens. He achieved his main goal, which was not only new true varieites but a "shaken-up" heredity that would ensure new combinations of qualities for future work.

It was typical of Burbank, to insist that he had not attained his ideal of a perfect plum—or, in fact, a perfect anything else. He wanted fruit that was better for its particular purpose than all others had ever been. Had he obtained a perfect plum, he was not sure he would have been pleased. "One does not really wish to reach the end of a trail," he argued, "leaving nothing to strive for, no unknown territory to explore." Part of the excitement, for him, of plant breeding, was that no one ever knew exactly what would be the result of any experiment.

Chapter 7

Fairer Flowers

To remind himself of the flower speckled, green hills of his boyhood home in Massachusetts, Burbank had brought with him to California some plants of the wild field daisy. It was a rugged little plant that bloomed abundantly all summer long. But he could never look at it without thinking of ways to make it more attractive.

First he grew the daisy in good rich soil, cultivated it well, and watched for improvements. But the daisy did not change much, so Burbank decided to cross it with other daisies that might add desirable qualities. He began a long series of experiments that lasted seventeen years—from 1884 till 1901.

There was an English daisy, he knew, that had larger flowers than the American daisy. It was weedy looking, but he hoped that by crossing it with the American daisy he could produce a plant that would combine the larger flowers of the English variety with the graceful abundant flowers and early blooming qualities of the American daisy. Burbank took pollen from the European daisy and placed it on the pistils of the best looking specimens of his American daisy.

In due time seeds formed, and these were sown. The plants grew and when it came to blooming time, Burbank inspected the blossoms carefully. It was always exciting to see what the new flowers from such a cross would be like. No two plants were identical, and it took keen eyes to detect differing qualities. Among the lot he found some that blossomed very early and abundantly, and just as he had hoped, with very large flowers.

Burbank then attempted to improve this hybrid plant further by crossing it with a German daisy that was just a bit different from the English one. This cross resulted in a slight improvement.

Six years passed; the best specimens selected from the thousands he had grown were superior daisies. They were rugged plants with large flowers which bloomed profusely through a long season. But they were still disappointing to Burbank, for to his sharp eyes, they had a slight yellowish tinge. Most people did not notice this, and saw no difference in the thousands of plants growing in his many rows.

Even Burbank's own gardener said "White is white, and all these daisies are white. They look the same color to me."

But Burbank answered, "Yes, white is white, there is no doubt about that. But these daisies are *not* white, and they do *not* look just alike to me. No one of them is pure white, but there is one that is nearer white than the rest, or else my eyes deceive me."

Many people were asked to look at the daisies and no one could see any difference among them. But when a San Francisco artist visited the gardens and was asked to pick the whitest of the plants, she picked the one that Burbank had always thought whiter than the rest.

This particular plant was selected for use in further experiments. Burbank decided that he needed a new cross to rid his prize plant of the last tinge of yellow that remained. It was then he learned of a Japanese daisy that had flowers of the purest white. He lost no time in getting seed from this Japanese plant. The plants that grew from these seeds were coarse looking, and had small flowers, but they were as white as white could be. He took pollen from the Japanese daisy and placed it on the pistils of the flowers of his prize plant. He grew thousands of plants from the seed of this cross, and finally selected one with all the good qualities of the previous crosses, plus the beautiful whiteness of the Japanese type.

From this remarkable plant, carrying the heredity

of Japanese, British, German and American daisies, thousands of plants were raised each year for nearly six years. From each crop, the best plants were selected, and all the others destroyed. Finally Burbank produced the wonderful flower known to this day as the *Shasta Daisy*. He named it after the snow-capped peak of the Sierras, Mount Shasta, which he could see in the distance above his special choice bed of daisies.

The popular Shasta combines the finest qualities of daisies from three continents with qualities no daisies ever had before. Its lovely, large, pure white flowers bloom abudantly all summer long. A campaign has been started, led by Californians, to have it named the national flower of the United States.

The Shasta Daisy was only one of many flowers with which Burbank worked. It was impossible for him to have a bed of flowers of any kind without his seeing possibilities of improving them. Even when he took walks on Sundays for relaxation, he marked flowers that looked exciting to him, so that he could return later and collect the ripened seeds. He usually marked them with strips of cloth or string, and when he ran out of these would tear up handkerchiefs or neckties or pull out the laces from his shoes to mark the plants that caught his attention. He said of himself, "On more than one occasion I was reduced to using a shoestring, and several times I labored home along a dusty road with my shoes flapping."

"There is one here that is nearer white than the rest."

When Burbank was asked, "What is your favorite flower?" he replied, "I have no favorite flower, except of course, the rose." He began experiments with roses in the 1880's, gathering specimens from all over the world and using them in crosses. He knew from the beginning that it would be difficult to achieve anything with roses, because they had already received so much attention from horticulturists everywhere. Nevertheless, he managed to introduce many fine varieties of hardy, everblooming roses. One of these was acclaimed the best bedding rose and was awarded a gold medal at the Louisiana Purchase Exposition at St. Louis, Missouri, in 1904. It was called the "Burbank" and was popular for many years.

With one flower, the amaryllis, Burbank worked to develop a size. Breeding for size was not a new idea. Burbank himself loved to tell the story of the Prussian King who attempted to develop a race of giants by selective breeding. The king marshaled all the tall men he could find into a special regiment of his army and then sent inspectors over the kingdom in search of tall women as wives for his tall soldiers. He intended to produce a royal bodyguard of giants that would be the astonishment of the world. Burbank thought this king was on the right track, but that his experiment would have had to go on for at least 250 years to produce a race of giants. He said: "If the project of the Prussian King, which was inaugurated about the middle of the eighteenth century, had been systematically followed up by his successors, there is a possibility that a ten-foot giant would have appeared among the descendants of the giant guardsmen about the year 2000 A.D."

In the case of the amaryllis, Burbank expected results in a much shorter time, for it took only three or four years for a whole new generation of amaryllis plants to produce new seed. It actually took Burbank ten generations of hybridizing and selecting to produce his new types of amaryllis. Several of his new amaryllis flowers had a ten-inch diameter, and were indeed giants among flowers.

The golden yellow poppy that covered California hills in the spring also drew Burbank's attention. One day he noticed that one of these plants had flowers with a fine line of red on one of its petals. He marked this plant, saved its seeds and planted them. Among the offspring the scarlet color was repeated, but it still showed only slightly. He kept selecting the seed of these flowers that showed the most red, until finally he produced a pure scarlet California poppy. He also developed one with white petals, and another with lemon-yellow edges and golden-yellow centers.

With the *gladiolus,* Burbank set out to strengthen stalks, enlarge flowers, and solidly mass the flowers on the stem, for even the best varieties from Europe had the flowers scattered on the stem and all on one side.

He wanted them to surround the stem like the flowers of the hyacinth. In a ten-year period he raised about a million hybrid seedlings, and from them selected those with the stiffest stems and the most densely crowded spikes of large flowers. In all, Burbank introduced over forty new varieties of gladioli. It is likely that all the gladioli bulbs sold and planted in America today are related to, or influenced by, one or another of Burbank's varieties.

It seemed to many people as though Burbank went along roadsides and gardens touching homely flowers with a magic wand and changing them into beautiful Cinderella-type plants. Actually, years and years of hard work, involving millions of plants, were necessary for the results he obtained. He conducted a constant search for plants with desirable qualities that he could merge with other desirable qualities in more common plants to produce the many fine varieties of flowers which he introduced to the world.

He took special pleasure in trying to introduce fragrance into flowers that had none, or that had positively disagreeable odors. "In any group of odorless flowers," he said, "you may have the good fortune to detect, if you search carefully enough, one that differs from its fellow in having at least a suggestion of fragrance. And if you will work in the right way with this individual, you will probably be able to produce a race of perfumed flowers."

He was able to introduce a sweet fragrance into a flower, the verbena, that had a rather disagreeable odor. Among the thousands of verbenas he had in his garden, a few had pleasant fragrances, especially in the evening. Burbank searched among these thousands of plants for one whose flowers had a pronounced perfume. Seeds from this plant were gathered and planted. From the new generation he selected some that were even more fragrant than their parents, and he continued selecting through succeeding generations until at least he had a plant as fragrant as could be wished.

With the calla lily, he was able to produce one with fragrant flowers very quickly, because after he found one plant with a lovely perfume, he was able to reproduce it by its underground tubers (enlarged parts of the stem).

He loved his lilies, for a time, above all his other plants. Once, when he had at least 250,000 distinct hybrids blooming among millions, he exclaimed, "Can my thought be imagined as I walk and look among these new forms of beauty, on which other eyes have never gazed!"

Chapter **8**

Adventures with Peas and Trees

There were few plants or trees of any kind that Burbank did not attempt to improve at one time or another. He worked on the sugar maple and on sugar cane. He worked on trees that give us rubber and turpentine, and on simple plants like rhubarb and chives. He worked on corn, wheat, oats and rye.

Everyone who ever visited Burbank commented on his modesty in describing his plant inventions. But he knew his accomplishments, and in respect to one feature of his work did not mind praising himself.

"Probably I was the first man who ever lived," he told his friend and biographer, Wilbur Hall, "to take a specific order for a new variety of plant or tree, and to deliver that order as definitely as a contractor, taking an architect's blueprints, will deliver a skyscraper or a church, a cottage or a mansion."

For example, he made to order a mulberry tree for a Japanese silk-grower. The grower wanted a tree that would produce twice as many leaves as food for silkworms than ordinary mulberry trees did. Having such a tree would mean, of course, that the grower could feed twice as many silkworms on the same amount of Japan's precious land. The tree also had to grow under the same conditions as existing mulberries in Japan and require no more fertilizer. Burbank worked complex experiments that took a long time, and then shipped grafts of the specified tree to Japan.

One day in 1904 he received a bigger challenge. A Western canner, J. H. Empson, came to him with the seemingly strange request for a particular kind of pea. It had to be small and sweet, like the *Petite Pois* of France, then a popular but expensive import in America. It had to be of uniform size, sweet, and all the peas had to mature at the same time so that the vines could be cut down at one time and the peas hulled by machinery.

"Do you think such a pea might be developed?"

"Certainly!" Burbank replied. "Will you give me the order?"

Mr. Empson laughed. "I would gladly place such a definite order if I thought you would accept it. But that is impossible, of course!"

"Not at all," Burbank replied. "I know what you want and will deliver it within eight years."

Empson told Burbank years later that he did not believe he was serious. Nevertheless, the contract was signed and Burbank went to work.

He planted a large field of carefully chosen peas. He selected the ones that came nearest the specifications called for, and planted again. It was a simple process, but required, as Burbank mused years later, "infinite pains and patience." As generations of selected peas passed through his hands, he counted the separate pods on each vine and the separate peas in each pod; quantity as well as quality was important. He soon found that he had made a mistake in his estimate of the time it would take. Thanks to the warm California climate he could raise two generations of peas in a year. In three years, or after the sixth generation, he sent Mr. Empson the following letter:

"By express today I send you all the peas raised from the *one best* of all my selections. This one is the one which produced the most peas to the pod, the most pods to the vines, had the most uniformly filled pods, and in all respects was the most productive and best: on the whole, the best pea, taking quality, quantity, and everything into consideration, which I have ever seen. They are fifteen percent smaller on the average. One other thing which I have added to them is that they are *sweeter* than the pea which you first sent me. They all came from *one single vine* which was the best in all respects and the seed has been reselected through six generations."

This letter was dated February 29, 1908. It took the company, of course, more years to reproduce enough peas to plant commercially. By 1912, however, exactly eight years after Mr. Empson's visit to Burbank, the company was able to plant hundreds of acres and supply the cannery with the small, sweet, uniform-sized and uniform-ripening peas they desired.

To the delight and amazement of Empson, Burbank refused to accept any payment, so well acquainted and friendly had they become during the course of Burbank's work on the pea. It was named the *Burbank-Empson,* and to this day some fifteen hundred to two thousand acres of them are grown and canned every year.

In his more than fifty years of work, there were few things Burbank didn't try on one plant or another, ranging from the most common weeds to the stately elm of New England villages or the trees of the forest.

Weeds had their own special reward. "What occupation can be more delightful," he asked, "than adopting the most promising individual from among a race of vile, neglected orphan weeds with settled hoodlum tendencies, downtrodden and despised by all, and gradually lifting it by breeding and education to a higher sphere?"

"What work can be more rewarding," he continued, "than to see it gradually change its sprawling habits, its coarse, ill-smelling foliage, its insignificant blossoms of dull color, to an upright plant with handsome, glossy, fragrant leaves, blossoms of every hue, and with a fragrance as pure and lasting as can be desired?"

"Plants are like children," he concluded. "Study their wants, help them to what they need, be endlessly patient, be honest with them, carefully correcting each fault as it appears, and in due time they will reward you bountifully for every care and attention, and make your heart glad in observing the results of your work."

Early in his work at Santa Rosa—in 1877—Burbank believed he saw possibilities for improving walnuts. He crossed an English walnut with a California black walnut, raised the seedlings, and selected the best. He planted six of these young trees along the street in front of his house, and gave them no irrigation or cultivation. The seedlings were planted in 1891. By 1905, the trees were nearly eighty feet tall, with trunks two feet through, and a branch spread of seventy-five feet. No man, living or dead had ever seen walnut trees grow like that. On the other side of the street were walnut trees that had been standing thirty years. They were fifteen feet high, with six-inch trunks.

Burbank named his new tree the "Paradox" and never ceased admiring it for its beauty, shade, rapid growth, and the quality of its wood for furniture, panelling, or burning in the fireplace. He also found in these trees an interesting example of a character hybrids often have. The first generation have extraordinary vigor, far beyond that of both their parents, but in successive generations the vigor is lost.

His "Royal" walnut was another hybrid, which like the "Paradox" was bred for shade and timber rather than its walnuts. It was a cross between the California black walnut and the New England black walnut. It not only turned out to be a noble tree, much larger than both its parents, but it produced excellent nuts, and so abundantly that a ton of nuts could be gathered from a single tree in one season. Some of Burbank's original plantings of 1885, are still living. One tree is a hundred feet tall with a branch spread of a hundred and twenty-five feet.

These two new walnut trees were not merely the product of hybridization. They were selected from the most rapidly growing seedlings of the thousands he raised. It required many years of work, but it opened up a new field never before explored, one which is only now being developed.

There were many who scoffed at the idea that trees could be improved. Once, while talking with an official of the national Department of Forestry, Burbank mentioned that the department's problems could best be met by developing new types of forest trees. The official found the suggestion weird and grotesque. The individual species of trees seemed so solidly and permanently established that few foresters were ready to accept the idea that forest trees could be hybridized to produce new types for faster growth, harder wood, and a more ornamental landscape. Today, seventy-five years after Burbank's idea of new forest species was greeted with sarcasm and derision, huge sums are being spent by private and government agencies to develop improved varieties of forest trees.

Burbank had predicted prophetically:

There is work enough to be done in this line for the government to put at work a thousand experts, and the possibilities ahead of them are so great that the whole face of nature might be changed by an intelligent, patient and systematic following of breeding and selection.

Burbank had worked on the walnut mainly to improve the size of the tree, but he also worked to improve the nuts. Chestnuts and paper-shell walnuts were his favorites. He produced chestnut trees that were dwarfed and so quick to mature that some actually bore nuts six months after the seeds germinated, and all were sure to produce nuts the second year after planting.

Even as a boy in Massachusetts, Burbank had noticed an unusual variation among chestnut trees. In gathering the nuts in the woods around Lancaster, he found that some trees bore large, glossy, sweet, brown nuts, while others had only small and inferior ones. This difference in the nuts, he recognized, was not due to local conditions, for trees standing side by side might sometimes bear extremely different chestnuts.

He remembered this fact when he began his experiments in California. He imported chestnuts from Japan, Italy and other countries. He crossed these with the best American types, including a California species called the *Chinquapin*. He interbred these various types in every possible way, often grafting many seedlings on a few trees to save precious space and to ease the work of fertilizing the flowers of one with the pollen of another. Sometimes he had several hundred chestnut grafts on the same tree. Some of his chestnuts combined the ancestral strains of the Japanese, European, and American chestnuts and the little California *Chinquapin*. He got some of these chestnut crosses to bear nuts the very first season. This was a big advantage, for it meant he could get new generations to experiment with each year.

Never satisfied, Burbank later spent considerable effort trying to get the spiny bur off the outside of the chestnut. He knew that the chestnut had a spineless bur and shell in remote ages, and that one of his strains was sure to show up with this characteristic.

At length, he got a partially spineless variety, but its nuts were not as good or as large as he wanted. He worked with this variety, confident that in future generations he could get a completely smooth-burred chestnut, and then he would be able to breed the good qualities of his best hybrid nuts into the combination.

It is difficult for people used to seeing grocery-store counters and bins piled high with nuts of many kinds to realize that these nuts were not produced commercially on a large scale until a generation or two ago. Before that they grew wild and were gathered in the woods. Burbank saw that nuts could constitute a valuable commercial crop if they were raised in huge orchards and shipped in large quantities to cities across the country. From 1895 to 1915, the commercial production of walnuts alone increased six-fold. His work on chestnuts, almonds, and hickory nuts also helped to increase production of these nuts.

Burbank saw that the American walnut that had to be cracked with a hammer would never gain in popularity. He therefore imported Persian or so-called English walnuts that had "paper-shells," with the aim of improving existing varieties. He knew that a walnut with a shell that could be crushed with the fingers would be popular at the dinner table.

His work on paper-shell walnuts was so successful that he soon developed one that had a shell so thin and soft that even birds could penetrate it with their bills. This became a disadvantage, and he found it desirable to breed it back to a thicker shell. His *Santa Rosa Soft Shell,* the final product of years of work, was introduced commercially in 1906.

Chapter 9

The Spineless Cactus

Shortly after the publication of his first "New Creations" catalog in 1893, Burbank began work on the cactus. Of all the plants he ever worked with, the cactus gave him the greatest pain physically, and the most headaches professionally. Many times he sadly regretted that he had ever tackled this "outcast warrior among plants." But Burbank had a vision of what he could do with the cactus of the desert. He saw it as a plant of enormous possible value.

He would remove its spines to make it a good forage plant for animals. It would grow luxuriantly, he thought, in dry places where nothing else would grow, and thus help to reclaim otherwise useless vast deserts in

Asia, Africa, Australia, and America. It would be hardy and resistant to extremes of temperature. Its fruits would be improved, so that men would find them delicious and tasty.

The biggest problem with the cactus was its spines. To develop a really useful cactus he had to get the spines off. Thinking of ways to do this led him to ask himself how the spines got there in the first place.

This is how he explained the cactus thorns: "One day it suddenly occurred to me that every desert plant is either bitter, poisonous, or spiny. The sagebrush is almost as irritant as a bee's sting; the euphorbia is as poisonous as a snake; the cactus as armored as a porcupine."

"There must be some reason for that bitterness," he thought, "that poison, those spines!"

"What other reason could there be?" he asked himself, "than that these are the plant's provisions for self-defense?"

"But," people often asked him, "you don't mean to say that nature gave these plants their spines, poision, and so on, to protect them from animals? Nature also made the animals that would starve if they didn't have plants to eat."

"It's not that simple," Burbank would reply. "I mean merely that if these desert plants hadn't developed extraordinary facilities for getting water, for holding the water they get against the fierce rays of the sun and the hot winds, and for preventing such animals as the antelope and the buffalo from eating them, they would never have survived. And for one species that survived, scores must have perished. It took thousands of nature's experiments and the death of millions of individuals to get just the right combination of qualities required for these plants to live under the exacting condition of the desert."

"Really to understand any plant, you see," Burbank would explain, "one has to look into its history. It became what it is now through its whole course of development. The North American cactus seems to have originated in an area that was once a great inland sea. This included parts of Nevada, Arizona, Utah and Northern Mexico. The deserts there now were once the bed of that sea. As the sea dried up, many plants had an opportunity to thrive. Among them was the cactus, which must have been an entirely different looking plant than the cactus of today. In the struggle for existence, those cacti with fewer and smaller leaves could hold their moisture better against the burning heat of the sun. Some plants had longer roots which enabled them to get the sub-soil moisture more easily. Some had thicker stalks. Those that had these qualities survived. The less favored perished.

"Then came the animals and new qualities were required for survival. Quite likely, many plants which had survived the evaporation of the sea and heat of the broiling sun failed to survive the new danger—the onslaught of the animals. The varieties of cactus that developed spines survived this new peril too, and in times spines became a central feature of their heredity."

Burbank conceived his task to be that of taking this plant backward to the time when it was spineless.

These desert plants, he recognized, had to survive under the most difficult conditions. They came through to the present time the hard way. Theirs was a struggle that only the tough and the hardy, the poisonous and the spiny could survive. The plants that we have nourished and protected for generations thrive because we have relieved them of the responsibility of defense and reproduction. "But no man," Burbank liked to say, "was ever kind to the cactus, cultivated the sagebrush, or cherished the euphorbia."

"You don't mean," one of his visitors once quipped, "that you got the thorns off the cactus by being kind to it?"

Burbank replied that it was not as simple as that. As the plants were here before there were animals to feed on and destroy them, there must have been a time in their history when they had no need of spines for their defense. He concluded that if the spines were acquired by these plants naturally, they could be gotten off again with effort and ingenuity.

But his guests sometimes asked him another question. If the spines were a development over the ages and if millions of individuals were eliminated in the process, how could Burbank expect to reverse all that in one short life-time with the limited number of specimens and generations he could handle?

"That's a good question," he would answer, "and don't think it didn't bother me. But I was sure I knew the answer. It was this: if the cactus has been transformed into a wild porcupine of a plant, then among all the thousands and more varieties of cacti there now are, I thought that by proper crossing and selection I could bring out and reinforce the original spinelessness."

One question that troubled people was whether Burbank's cactus, too, would not in time develop spines for the same reason its ancestors did. Burbank understood that the same reason could not exist. Under the conditions in which the spines developed, nature selected for survival those that had the most spines. Or, in other words, animals destroyed them less often. Now, on the contrary, man would eliminate those that showed a tendency towards spines. Of all new plants, only the spineless would be selected and given preferential treatment for survival.

Burbank started his work on the cactus by collecting hundreds of varieties. A special collection came from Washington, and specimens were sent him from Mexico, South America, Hawaii, France, and Sicily. Most of these proved useless, but he tried them all, crossing them in countless ways. Armed with a camel hair brush, again and again he placed pollen from one cactus flower on a watch crystal and dusted it on the stigma of another flower. After the seeds developed, he planted them by the thousand, and selected plants that had the desired qualities. He crossed again, and selected again until he had what he wanted.

It took him nine years to get a cactus absolutely free of spines. But the plants still had clusters of hundreds of tiny spicules and it took more time to get rid of them.

"The whole thing was the most soul-testing experience I have ever undergone," Burbank told his friends in later years.

"For five years or more the cactus blooming season was a period of torment to me both day and night. Time and again I wished with all my heart I had never touched the cactus to attempt to remove its spines. Not only would the little spicules find lodging everywhere in my skin, but my clothing would become filled with them and they would work their way through the cloth and into my flesh, causing intense irritation."

Finally, Burbank got rid of the spines and spicules, but it took six more years to improve the fruit and make the cactus hardier.

Then he ran into a difficulty. It was harder go get the spineless cactus started in arid areas than he had anticipated, because squirrels and rabbits and other small animals ate up the young, smooth cactus plants. The plants had to be fenced until they got thoroughly rooted, and the original slab developed a tough bark. This was often a difficult and expensive, if not impossible task.

Once the cactus plants did not have spines to protect them, Burbank learned, man has to protect them against the animals or they cannot get started. He saw that the plants most useful to man are likely to require man's aid to survive and reproduce. Taking away the cactus spines that had protected the plant through the ages created new problems for man as well as new possibilities.

In spite of all the physical pain it had given him, Burbank was fonder of his spineless cactus than anything else he produced. He took thousands of visitors through his gardens showing them his pet varieties—he had produced some 69 new varieties in all. One had a high food value for grazing animals. Another grew with great rapidity. Others were noted for their juiciness, and still others for their delicious fruit. Henry Ford, Thomas Edison, the Dutch botanist Hugo de Vries, the great pianist Ignace Paderewski, and other famous people were impressed, but Burbank enjoyed most showing his spineless *Opuntia* to Helen Keller. Her fingers, sensitive from reading braille through a lifetime of blindness, especially appreciated the smooth velvety slabs of this once spiny cactus.

The extraordinary reproductive powers of the cactus always fascinated Burbank. Any slab could be cut off his *Opuntia* varieties and grow a whole new plant. He once absentmindedly left a slab in an overcoat pocket. To his amazement it developed roots. He loved to point to the eyes of his cactus slabs. Some had as many as

"This crate of cacti built and furnished my new home."

fifty different ones, and each was capable, under the right conditions, of developing into either a root, a new slab, or a fruit.

A California writer, Honoria Tuomey, recalled a visit to Burbank after he had finished work on the cactus.

He received her in his new home, just completed, then led her across the street to his old house. On the back stoop was a plain pine box, smaller than the crate for a five-gallon can of gasoline. She read the label: "Mr. John M. Rutland, Melbourne, Australia. Live Plants. Keep from Frost and Heat, Luther Burbank, Santa Rosa, Sonoma Co., California."

The expressman was about due to call for it and Burbank explained to his visitor: "The contents of that box built and furnished the new house. Seven of those cactus leaves [slabs] sold for thirty-five hundred dollars, and the eighth, an extra fine one named the 'Santa Rosa,' for one thousand dollars. The thirty-five hundred dollars built the house, and the thousand dollars furnished it."

This single sale, of course, did not begin to pay for the cost of producing the new cactus. But in ensuing years Burbank sold nurserymen fifty tons of slabs and plants, with the rights to reproduce and market them in given areas. Rutland, an Australian nurseryman who had been an old customer of Burbank, had bought, along with his eight slabs, sole marketing rights for the southern hemisphere.

Unfortunately, the spineless cactus gave Burbank as many heart and headaches as the spiny ones had given him skin itches. He himself had great confidence in it, and the nurserymen to whom he sold it outdid one another to make extravagant claims about it. The United States

Department of Agriculture got a flood of inquiries concerning the new cactus. They were wary of recommending new plants until they had been well proven. The Department took the stand that cactus of any kind, spiny or spineless, was at best only an emergency crop for years of extreme drought. They also said that without irrigation and cultivation its yields would not be what Burbank and the nurserymen who were marketing the cactus claimed. Finally, the Department pointed out that the cactus had to be protected by fencing, thus making it a farm, rather than a range or desert crop.

The battle raged for nearly ten years after Burbank's first announcements of new cacti in 1903. David Griffiths, cactus expert of the U. S. Department of Agriculture, made extensive researches into its usefulness. He found that like all other plants, it would not grow without water, even though it could remain alive without water much longer than most plants. It required at least a short rainy season. Burbank, himself, had to advertise in 1912 that some dealers were misrepresenting the amount of cold his cactus could withstand. It could withstand, he said, short periods of freezing temperatures, but not climates where the soil froze an inch or more in depth.

Claims and counter-claims ran rampant. David Fairchild, famous plant explorer, had sent four forms of spineless cactus to Burbank from Argentina, Sicily, Tunis and Ceylon. Fairchild was shocked at announcements that Burbank had made the only spineless one in the world. But Burbank claimed only that his was *better* than any of the others—than any found in nature—larger and more suitable for forage. Dairymen claimed that Burbank's cactus was a good supplemental feed for milk cows. His friends and admirers leaped to his defense.

The controversy finally narrowed to one between Burbank and Griffiths, the cactus specialist of the Department of Agriculture. Bitterness increased when dealers, who had paid high prices to Burbank for his cactus, continued to push sales against government opposition. Did this practice have Burbank's blessing? Many officials believed it did, and they raised questions about Burbank's integrity and loyalty to scientific truth.

In 1909 the subsidy that had been given Burbank every year since 1904 by the Carnegie Institution was withdrawn, even though it was to run for five more years. Both supporters and opponents of Burbank believed the cactus controversy was a big factor in this decision. So hot did the fight grow that in 1912 a California congressman introduced a bill in Washington authorizing the Department of the Interior to set apart some 7,680 acres of land in one of the semi-desert states for further experiments by Burbank with his cactus. The bill was passed by the House of Representatives but never got through the Senate.

Whether Burbank actually wanted such a bill passed

is not known. Looking back, it seems likely that Burbank exaggerated the possibility of cactus as a food for man and animal and as a means of reclaiming desert lands. Yet, that he made many improved varieties, at great physical and economic cost, is incontestable. Perhaps he came to love, too much, this "warrior among plants." One other possibility, however, remains—that because of the fight over its merits, and the high prices resulting from speculation by dealers, it has never been properly tried out.

It may be that Burbank's spineless cactus for forage and his other spineless varieties yielding improved fruit were not everything he believed they were. Perhaps he had devoted so much time and labor to it and became so intoxicated with ideas of what it could be and do, that he became unable to view his results objectively.

Chapter 10

Growth of a Legend

During more than a quarter of a century, beginning about 1900, Burbank was not only a man but a legend. In the course of those years, the legend grew to staggering proportions. And as the legend grew, it has been said, his gardens became almost a shrine, and to shake hands with him a benediction.

Millions of Americans had found a new hero. What could be more appropriate in an America lighting its houses with electricity, and taking to the roads in "flivers," or "Model-T's," than that plants, too, should be modernized by being made bigger, better, and more serviceable to man? It was an age in which anything seemed possible.

The story is told of a woman, who seeing for the

first time a kangaroo with its baby's head sticking out of its pouch, exclaimed "What will they think up next!" That was very much the way Burbank's successive announcements of new varieties was greeted by millions of Americans. A "white blackberry," a spineless cactus, a plant that grew potatoes under the ground and tomatoes above (a graft, of course, that could not be propagated), and such wonders, came to be expected as a matter of course. As the Governor of California said, at a dinner in Burbank's honor in 1905, "New fruits, new flowers, new trees seem to spring into being obedient to his Aladdin-like touch."

No one thought it strange when the newspapers carried the story of a request sent Burbank by the President of an Irish patriotic society asking him to make the shamrock, the Irish national emblem, grow a flower that would be a worthy symbol of Irish freedom. The letter to Burbank indicates the image of him which existed in the minds of so many people. "Of you," it read in part, "whose metamorphic creations in the world of plants and flowers have startled all who have seen or read of them, we would inquire as to the possibilities of redeeming from the downtrodden and wild soil the hardy and delicate emblem of the Irish nation. What might a horticulturist hope to produce from the Irish trefoil? Could its present elegant but diminutive blossom be transformed into a real and attractive flower?"

Burbank had a secretary to answer the hundreds and thousands of letters he received of this kind. In this particular case, the inquirer was told that Burbank had worked on the shamrock some years earlier but gave it up in the belief that no one "will be able to give it a bloom really worthy of the Celtic national flower."

On another occasion, when a Georgia planter told newspapers it would be possible to grow black cotton, *The New York Times* wired Burbank for his opinion. Burbank wired back that it wasn't an absolute impossibility by any means, but it seemed somewhat doubtful to him if black cotton would be produced "during this generation, if ever." And he concluded his telegram with: "My congratulations to the man who shall produce black cotton!"

Burbank's modesty with respect to the shamrock flower and black cotton did not at all detract from the legend. Ever since the first issue of "New Creations," and especially after 1901 when journalists began to make capital of Burbank, the belief spread that he could produce anything he set his mind to. He was called "King of Horticulture," as well as "Wizard." He even became "the Columbus who has opened a new world." Weeds became "neglected orphans," simply plants that Burbank had not yet gotten around to improving. Once, in Philadelphia, when a buyer of the "Burbank Rose" asked who this man was who had roses named for him, it was solemnly explained that he was the man who discovered the potato while trying to take the offensive odor out of garlic and onions without spoiling their flavor.

The story of the Burbank potato had spread and become completely fantastic. But it dove-tailed neatly with another popular legend. It was said that Thomas Edison had spilled chemicals on the floor of a baggage car, was fired from his job as a train boy, and made electricity his vocation. Luther Burbank found a seed-ball in his mother's potato patch—so the story ran—and became the world's greatest inventor of new plants. The Horatio Alger books, so popular at that same time, told the stories of poor but virtuous boys who always made good. As fanciful as these books were, they could not hold a candle to the Edison and Burbank legends. It was no accident that a letter from Austria, addressed simply, "Burbank, Botanist and Scientific Planter, U.S. Nordamerika," promptly reached its destination in Santa Rosa, California.

The legend of Burbank as a wonder worker was heightened by the jokesters and professional comedians of the time. Burbank squirmed at some of the jokes, but he knew people were laughing *with* him, not *at* him. The humorists said he had crossed the eggplant with the milkweed to make an omelette plant, and that he had made rhubarb pie by crossing rhubarb and wheat. As corny as these jokes were, they are an index of Burbank's enormous popularity as well as testimony to the fact that he brought the concepts of hybridization and the idea of new plant varieties into virtually every American home.

Once, however, he found a magazine article under the title, "Burbank versus Nature."

"I can't remember anything that made me quite so hot under the collar," he confided to a friend. "It was something like writing a treatise called: 'Wilbur and Orville Wright versus the Law of Gravitation.' ". The very thing on which Burbank most prided himself was his knowledge of nature and his diligence in following her laws.

For a time a new term came into being part of the American language. It was "to Burbankize," and it meant to improve plants by hybridization and selection. Warning was given, though, that not everyone could expect to Burbankize successfully, because few people had Burbank's "acute vision, remarkable color sense, and almost abnormally developed senses of smell and taste." Writers pictured him walking through beds of thousands of flowers, picking out one among them all as the whitest, another as the largest, and so on. It is true that Burbank was especially gifted in sense discrimination. But writers for newspapers and popular magazines claimed he had super-human qualities, and the staidest newspaper editorials spoke of his "almost uncanny intelligence."

Much damage was done to the true story about Burbank by such articles. He once exclaimed in exasperation, "The extravagant estimates of my work have been the bane of my existence and there has been much written about me by sensational writers who know nothing either of me or my work. I am not responsible for all these things and anyone with any knowledge of horticulture could discern at once that much of the stuff sent out is nothing but the space-writer's chaff."

To the exaggerated magazine and newspaper articles were added the exaggerated claims of dealers. The nursery business was a highly competitive one, and nurserymen were not accustomed to understating the merits of their products. Nursery firms vied with one another to get new Burbank offerings on their lists, and they praised these offerings to the skies.

Then in 1905 a hero-worshipping author, W. S. Harwood, published the first full-length book on Burbank, entitled "New Creations in Plant Life." This work "fixed" the Burbank legend for years to come, even though many of Burbank's best friends regretted that it was ever published.

Harwood's style was not unusual for a time when there were heroes in the land, and authors only too happy to cater to the popular taste of hero worship. A chapter labeled, "A Day with Mr. Burbank," closed with the following picture:

When the evening comes, it is a worn and tired figure that curls up upon a low couch in his little living-room—tired physically, no less than mentally, many a time worn to the very verge of exhaustion. An hour or so he lies silently resting, not asleep, for his mind is eternally turning upon the work before him. . . . Yet all the days in this man's life are rich in the splendid consciousness of duty done, glorified by the joy of having helped the great primal forces of Nature to help mankind.

To this picture of a superman the author added a quotation from the Newark, New Jersey, *News.*

Luther Burbank—until recently an unknown name—has bestowed upon the world a greater increment of values, in things done and things inevitable, which are for the permanent betterment of civilization, than any score of celebrities in this decade or in any previous decade or century, when the fact is submitted to ultimate analysis. He has produced more new plant-life, fruits, grasses, trees and flowers, than any other man who has ever lived. . . .

The reflex of all future achievement will throw back its glory to brighten Burbank's aureole, for he will have been the master and protagonist. Is it too much to say that among the great benefactors of their race Luther Burbank will be unique in the splendor of his monument? That can never crumble while sunshine, air and soil carry on their chemistry.

This was an impossible order for any man to live up to, and it was just as impossible to live it down. Is it any wonder that visitors to Santa Rosa, who had been fed on such fantastic glorifications of a hero, were often taken aback when they caught a glimpse of Burbank over the low picket fence that surrounded his gardens? To their amazement, they saw only an ordinary-looking man, no bigger than the average, and with no halo over his head.

In 1906, the year of the great San Francisco earthquake, the Burbank legend achieved a new and alarming dimension. In a few seconds the quake leveled to the ground the whole business section of Santa Rosa. Damage was widespread on all sides. But, as the press diligently reported, no damage whatever was done to Burbank's greenhouse or any of his plants. The devastating earthquake left Burbank and his work untouched. To some this appeared nothing short of miraculous. It strengthened the mystical belief that he was a kind of superman.

Long before Burbank's death, his life was being handed down to millions of school children as a sort of

Washington-Lincoln hybridization. Fairy tales spun about him struck the fancy of old and young alike. Teachers on the look-out for heroes to hold up as models for their children found the Burbank legend ready-made for their purpose. He was everything they needed in the days when the Alger books were still popular. Here was a "Phil the Fiddler," or a "Paul the Peddler," in real life. He had all the necessary virtues for the "poor boy who made good." He never drank nor smoked. He was a perfect example of the idea of *service* as opposed to self-seeking. He was the humanitarian carried to perfection.

His improved plants, it was said, had made food more abundant and lowered the cost of living. Coupled with this was the widely publicized claim that he was a "wizard" who could work "wonders" and was gifted with the "magical art of producing new fruits and flowers." It is no wonder that he was held up as an inspiration to the youth of the country.

One of the most remarkable things about the Burbank legend is the length of time it lasted. For a full twenty-five years he lived in the limelight. A lesser man might have lost his head, but Burbank took it all in his stride, making fun of the absurd inventions of space writers.

On the one hand, Burbank chaffed under the legend and knew that many features of it were doing him no good. On the other hand, the continuation of his experimental work required an ever-growing reputation. And while he shunned the limelight in person, he loved the adulation that he thought was his due. The successive birthdays of "California's most famous citizen" were events the whole country noted. And on New Year's Day the press services carried round the world stories such as: "With the completion of one of the busiest years in his half-century of work in the laboratory of nature, Luther Burbank today presented to the world as a New Year's gift a beautiful group of new flowers and plants."

Burbank made horticulture spectacular. He stirred the imagination of masses by demonstrating that plants could be changed and improved in desired directions. In the eyes of millions, Burbank's work in his experimental gardens held out the hope and promise of a better and fairer future for mankind.

Chapter 11

Burbank and the Scientists

A sharp and bitter debate centered about Burbank for many years. In spite of the legend, there were doubters who denied he did anything new. There were scientists who did not doubt that he accomplished many wonderful things, but questioned whether he accomplished them scientifically. These critics bothered Burbank the most.

"He doesn't keep proper records of his crosses and their offspring," some scientists said accusingly.

Burbank retorted: "When something like seven and a half million plum seedlings passed under my hand and eye in my experiments to perfect this fruit, is it any wonder I didn't record each individual cross?"

Again, university professors said: "Look at the crazy

claims dealers make for Burbank's productions, and he allows them to do it."

To this, Burbank replied: "Can I help it if a dealer to whom I sell a good, thoroughly tested, new plant tells his customers things I never claimed for it?"

Sometimes it was found that Burbank's plants did not do as well in different soils and climates as they did in Santa Rosa. His answer could be only that until other people and institutions tried his plants under all kinds of circumstances there was no way of knowing just how they would do.

Some professors of horticulture claimed it was absurd for anyone to try to do as much as Burbank did. "Only an institution," they protested, "not an individual, can carry on such extensive experiments."

To this, Burbank retorted: "If more people used my large-scale methods of selection and hybridization, the orchards and gardens of this country would have many more fine varieties in them than they have today."

"Look!" some scientists observed, "Burbank doesn't have a single assistant who is a college graduate." They intimated that it was because he did not want anyone watching him who had better scientific training than he had.

Burbank accepted the first part of this charge. "I have never been able to make use of a college graduate," he admitted. "Those who aid me must come with receptive rather than schooled minds. They must bring sympathetic, as distinct from reluctant or doubting hands."

And then, after every such round of criticism, the failure to keep proper records would come up again. Once Burbank exploded: "Records! A flea might as well undertake to write down the number of jumps he makes a day on a healthy dog!"

The argument was hopeless. On one side, the trained scientists found Burbank's methods sloppy and careless. Secondly, he was accused of not knowing enough about heredity and environment, about species and varieties. Why, he even claimed to have crossed plants of two different species (the raspberry and the blackberry, for example) and obtained from the cross offspring that were fertile and produced fruits and seeds that could reproduce. Every scientist was sure, in the years around 1900, that species were distinguished most decisively by the fact that, like the mule—the cross of a donkey and a horse—hybrids are incapable of begetting offspring.

Burbank simply shurgged his shoulders and said, "I did it." Then he explained, "I don't mean to say that I did anything contrary to natural law, but merely that your so-called scientific definition of species is artificial and arbitrary." And he concluded with the venemous remark, "Nature doesn't conform to the requirements of science text-book writers."

His bonfires annoyed professional scientists no end.

Burbank's 1894 "New Creations" catalog contained a picture of sixty-five thousand hybrid raspberry-blackberry bushes which were to be consigned to the flames. Of forty thousand of one kind, he kept only one bush. Of twenty-five thousand of another crossing, he saved two dozen bushes for further trial.

Most people saw in these figures the fabulous work required to produce a new race of berries. But trained botanists, for very good reasons, saw in this bonfire only "a vast amount of scientific data sent up in smoke." The fact was that Burbank did not even speak the language of the scientific botanist. The scientific botanists, on the other hand, probably never realized that he didn't really care to. He had his own task to perform and knew what was needed to perform it.

When an occasional scientist from a university or a research institute visited Burbank, he was shocked that Burbank had no library. There were only a few books on his shelves. Besides his favorite volumes of Darwin, his chief guides in technical botanical matters were Asa Gray's *First Lessons in Botany* and *Field, Forest and Garden Botany*. When he was asked what text he would recommend to interest youth in nature study, he replied, with a twinkle, "I thank my lucky stars that I was never taught the old-fashioned form of botany in school."

Beneath the surface of such glib and partly truthful replies, however, lay the consciousness of his own limited training and perhaps a certain envy of those who had vastly more knowledge of botanical details than he had. Burbank perhaps was envious that scientists accepted Edison as one of them. Even before Burbank's first issue of "New Creations" in 1893, two books had been published on Edison who was only a few years his senior. Edison was a member of the National Academy of Sciences and had been given honorary doctorates in science, philosophy, and letters. Yet, like Burbank, Edison had had no formal scientific training. Perhaps this fact explains Burbank's delight at being accepted by Edison in later years as his equal in the realm of invention. Burbank loved to say that Edison's whole life had been spent in the same university as his, the university of nature.

Then, suddenly, between 1902 and 1904, the scientific world reluctantly began to acknowledge Burbank's contributions. In 1902, David Fairchild visited him. Fairchild was then a noted plant explorer who had traveled the earth in search of new plants that might be usefully grown in the United States. He had great influence with the Department of Agriculture in Washington and in many scientific circles.

Fairchild found himself "bewildered" by the magnitude of his host's planting operations. He wrote of "an old apple tree on which a thousand sorts of seedling apples had been grafted," of "rows of Japanese plums, forty thousand different seedlings he had grown," of a bed he was shown of "two hundred thousand flowering bulbs," and so on.

Driving in Burbank's little buggy back to Santa Rosa from the Sebastopol gardens, Burbank and Fairchild talked over the idea of getting an institution to support Burbank so that he could be relieved entirely of the nursery or marketing end of his business.

The following year, one of the most gratifying events in Burbank's whole career occurred when the California Academy of Science struck a gold medal in his honor: "in recognition of his notable services to mankind." Yet he was still not really accepted by most scientists.

Then recognition came from an unexpected quarter. The world-famous Dutch botanist, Hugo De Vries, professor at the University of Amsterdam, crossed the Atlantic and the continent to meet Burbank and to see for himself what Burbank was doing and how he did it. The two men had corresponded previously and De Vries knew enough of Burbank's work to fear that in the month of July, the only time he could get to California, Burbank would be too busy selecting prunes from his three hundred thousand different varieties to have much time to speak with him.

When De Vries reached San Francisco he found several other professors who wished to join him in a visit to Burbank. They were all invited to Santa Rosa to spend a night and a day. De Vries was entranced by Burbank, who to his surprise looked more like a gardener than a scholar, and who kept them in constant laughter, for he was full of life and fun. De Vries never forgot that re-

Burbank showed the professors a graft he was making.

markable visit. Burbank showed them everything he was working on and explained everything. They discussed the whole gamut of evolutionary theory, including genetic mutations—De Vries' special contribution to Darwinism —and the laws of heredity discovered by the Austrian monk, Gregor Mendel, which De Vries had only recently rediscovered.

Yet, for De Vries there was one disappointment. Burbank, he found, was playing "a game of solitaire on a large scale." The aim of De Vries' scientific studies was the origin and nature of new characters in plants. Burbank's experiences threw little or no light on this question. In a typical American way he tried everything and stuck by what worked. He had no secrets De Vries found. He merely worked on a larger scale than any person, firm or institution had every dreamed of doing before, and had "a great genius and an almost incredible capacity for work."

Before De Vries sailed for home, he spoke at a banquet in his honor in San Francisco. There he told an audience of scientists and interested laymen what he thought of Burbank. Here, for the first time, was a famous scientist and an objective observer giving Californians his evaluation of their most distinguished citizen.

"The flowers and fruits of California," he told them, "are less wonderful than the flowers and fruits which Mr. Burbank has made. He is a great and unique genius." There must have been considerable pride stirred in some, and shock in others when the biggest man in evolutionary theory since Charles Darwin told them that only one possessing genius of a high order could have such a knowledge of nature and such ability to handle plant-life.

The ordinary Californian had believed this for quite a while, but now scientists and university people generally could no longer ignore his genius. He could be passed over no more as merely a clever nurseryman who had extraordinary gifts of self-promotion. He might still be a gardener, but was now one touched with genius. Scientists had to take notice of him.

University scientists and scientific institutions now began to give Burbank attention, but unfortunately this gave him more headaches and heartaches than satisfaction. He and the scientists could not work together. He was playing a game of solitaire, and doing it in ways that violated all the standards of professional botanists.

Two important new avenues to Burbank as a scientists were opened, at least in part, by the visit of De Vries. The following year, 1905, he was appointed honorary lecturer on plant-breeding at Leland Stanford Jr. University, at the initiative of David Starr Jordan, its chancellor, and Professor Vernon Kellogg. Both these men had their interest aroused in Burbank by De Vries' enthusiastic report, and both spent some days with him at Santa Rosa. The honorary lectureship involved only two lectures a year to advanced students and professors. In these appearances, Burbank exhibited some of his new creations and explained his experiments.

But Burbank's biggest venture into the realm of conventional science came in another way the same year.

The Carnegie Institution of Washington decided to provide him with a cash subsidy of ten thousand dollars a year for ten years.

Burbank had become a scientist in spite of himself. No one knows just how this generous grant was decided upon, but it brought a storm of protest from university scientists. Burbank was not a scientist, they insisted, and he could show no scientific results from his experiments. The Carnegie Institution replied by promising to send a competent man to collaborate with Burbank and to see that he followed accepted procedures and kept his records straight.

The Carnegie Institution had been founded only three years earlier by the steel king, Andrew Carnegie, with an initial endowment of ten million dollars. Its declared purpose was "to encourage in the broadest and most liberal manner investigation, research and discovery and the application of knowledge to the improvement of mankind." Burbank seemed a natural for the Institution's Grant No. 221.

The Institution's Year Book for 1905 reported on Burbank's work then in progress:

A partial list of the plants upon which work is now progressing includes 300,000 new hybrid plums, the work of the past twenty-five years in crossing about every known species, and about ten thousand seedlings of the year's

growth; 10,000 new apples; many thousand
peach and peach-nectarine crosses; 8000 new
seedlings of pineapple quince; 400 new cherry
seedlings; 1000 new grapevines; 8000 new
hybrid chestnuts, crosses of American, Japa-
nese, Chinese, and Italian species . . . many
thousand apricots and plumcots . . . very
numerous other fruits in less numbers, and
10,000 new, rare, hybrid seedling potatoes.

This account sounded truly Burbankian, but there was a note that might have given Burbank and his close friends cause for alarm. It said that "much valuable material for thought will undoubtedly be found in the scientific account of the experiments" and that a trained biologist was being sought to prepare "a scientific account of the ways, means, methods, and results of Mr. Burbank's work." Everyone who knew Burbank at all well could have predicted the troubles he would have with a "trained scientist" following his every move. They could also have predicted the troubles a scientist would have keeping up with Burbank and getting him to explain, from morning till night, and day after day, every step that he was taking, and why.

One trained biologist proved not to be enough. In the next few years various experts were added to give assistance, and more were sought. Then it began to be evident that Burbank's experiments were often uncontrolled and his records sketchy.

The whole business proved most unfortunate for both parties. Burbank thought he was being subsidized to get more plants and make more wholesale crosses. The Institution directors thought they would collect a large amount of detailed information on the crosses he made, the exact parentage of every hybrid over many successive generations.

Such information would, indeed, have been invaluable for the formal study of genetics. Seldom, if ever, had there been such an extraordinary opportunity to study the mechanics of heredity. Mendel's work constituted the classic and precise model, but he worked only with one plant—the common garden pea—of which he studied only a few characters, while Burbank worked with thousands of varieties of plants and was concerned with changing half a dozen or more characters of each them at once.

The amazing thing is that the Carnegie grant and the collaboration between Burbank and a scientific geneticist lasted as long as it did. The chief scientist, Dr. George H. Shull, found Burbank "an individualist from start to finish." Dr. Shull obviously had a very difficult time working with Burbank and understanding the drive behind his work. Burbank wanted only to improve plants. Dr. Shull wanted more knowledge of the laws of heredity. After five years of the Carnegie relationship and after fifty thousand dollars had been paid to Burbank, the subsidy was ended, to the hurt of both Burbank's pride and his income.

To Burbank the whole episode was one of constant annoyance and interference with the way he was accustomed to doing things. As for the Institution's feelings, little or nothing is known, except that for five years more they continued to announce that Dr. Shull's report was still being prepared.

A terrible battle erupted between Burbank and his followers and the President of the Carnegie Institution. Burbanks' admirers demanded an explanation for the termination of the contract. The Institution refused to make any statement or to issue any report of any kind. Burbank, in a catalog issued in 1911, gave his version of his sad adventure among the scientists. "Yes," he wrote, he had been captured for five years by the Carnegie Institution for the "benefit of science." These were, he continued, "five years of care, leanness, hampering restrictions and unprofitable conditions, and having dictated to and corrected for their botanists several thousand pages, it is a most gracious relief to return to a life free from the red tape of institutional restrictions. . . ." The self-reliant individualist simply could not work under institutional conditions.

Dr. Shull's report of his five years of work with Burbank was never published. Apparently, it was never even written. Yet, thirty years later, he wrote of Burbank, "I always felt that he was the sort of man who *deserved* to be a popular hero."

Burbank, after the breakdown of the Carnegie grant, became more conscious than ever of the gap between him and college-trained scientists. "My schools," he would say, "have been only the University of Nature." And he added, "I matriculated in the College of Horticulture, Department of Market Gardening, but I finished that course in a short time and entered the laboratory where Nature teaches Plant Breeding." He always added that he hadn't graduated from that branch of the institution yet.

The lack of understanding between Burbank and the scientists lay in the tremendous gap that has existed through most of history between those with formal academic training and those trained through practical experience. It was also an indication of the gap between pure or theoretical science and science as applied in industry and technology. The cause of his difficulty with the scientists was not all Burbank's. Burbank and the scientists had different backgrounds, different aims, and lived in different environments. Many years later, one academic observer noted an important difference between his life and that of Burbank. "Institutional scientists," this retired professor commented, "as a rule do not have to worry unduly about where the money is coming from to support their laboratories and pay their salaries. Burbank had to make his discoveries pay all the expenses of his home, gardens, and greenhouse, and if there was anything left he might call it a salary."

Two university men stuck by Burbank through all the controversies over the years. They were Vernon Kellogg and David Starr Jordan of Stanford University. They admired him and deeply respected his work, in spite of his "unorthodox" methods. In 1905, at a complimentary banquet to Burbank given by the California Board of Trade, President Jordan expressed the congratulations to Burbank of both his University and the University of California. "We honor him as a man of our kind, the kind the university likes to make; the kind of men to whom Nature is an open book, and whose reading of this book is clear and truthful." Four years later Jordan and Kellogg published a small volume entitled: *Scientific Aspects of Luther Burbank's Work*. They never retreated from the position they took that, "If his place is outside the temple of science, there are not many of the rest of us who will be found fit to enter."

Chapter 12

Speculators and Promoters

If Burbank fared badly at the hands of the scientists, he fared still worse as a result of the efforts of promoters and speculators. Burbank became fair prey for all kinds of schemers. His genuine achievements, together with his fabulous popularity with a vast public, seemed to encourage exaggerated advertising and fantastic claims. They also attracted a wide assortment of promoters who sought to capitalize on Burbank's name and fame.

By 1912 Burbank had had many offers to take in partners. But in the spring of that year he contracted to sell all his creations, past, present and future, in what was called "one of the biggest deals of its kind in the world." A group of businessmen set up the "Luther

Burbank Company of San Francisco," which was henceforth to market all his products. Now Burbank would be able, supposedly, to devote himself entirely to creative work, no longer having to worry about selling anything to anybody.

The whole venture proved a colossal failure. Burbank had very little stock on hand of his old creations. His new ones would require several seasons to reproduce sufficient quantities for a big market. The people who founded the company were not experienced horticulturists, and they were inept at planting and testing his new creations. So, instead of getting cash for the sale of new plants, Burbank got only promissory notes.

The Luther Burbank Company made the most sensational claims in advertising his products, and everyone thought that in dealing with the company they were dealing with Burbank himself. It was simply taken for granted that the company was organized and controlled by Burbank, that it *was* Burbank, in fact. Many irate customers later accused Burbank of fraud and deceit.

Finally, in 1915 the Luther Burbank Company was forced into bankruptcy when Burbank brought suit against them to recover money due him on their promissory notes. His attorney claimed that he had been the victim of "stock pirates."

Burbank not only lost considerable money, but suffered considerable loss of reputation as well. The old established nursery companies had proven to be the best outlets, after all, through which his products could be marketed. There was no alternative for him but to stay in business, announcing his new varieties to established firms and seeking to get the best prices he could for them.

In an age of growing big business, Burbank's kind of individual enterprise on a large scale had become increasingly difficult. Thomas Edison was not only an inventor but a promoter, organizer, and skilled business man. He was able to build corporations around him, hire trusted lieutenants, and achieve considerable wealth. Burbank had moved into the twentieth century with the individualistic outlook of the days of Emerson and Thoreau. He needed large sums of money for his work, yet he insisted on doing everything by himself and in his own way. His predicament, while largely due to his own methods, ideals, and aims, was unfortunate and somewhat tragic. Things were just not being done his way in twentieth-century America.

The second Burbank promotion scheme took an entirely different form, but it was equally diastrous to his reputation. The same year the Burbank Company was formed, a representative of a Minneapolis publishing firm organized the Luther Burbank Press. The purpose of this organization was to publish a monumental set of volumes that would present the whole story of Burbank's life and work. It was a grandiose scheme for cashing in on the Burbank legend and his fabulous popularity.

The promoters needed capital, so they launched a bond issue of three hundred thousand dollars to supplement the six hundred thousand dollars worth of stock originally subscribed "by a group of prominent people from all over the United States." At the same time they solicited memberships in the Luther Burbank Society, involving the down payment of one dollar and an agreement to buy all ten projected volumes at fifteen dollars each as they came off the press. Prestige was the chief bait used to attract subscribers. Those invited were told that they were distinguished people, selected from among the most important in the United States. Naturally, memberships poured in, for who except sceptical scientists or disappointed customers would not want to join a society linked to the name of Burbank, even at the cost of one hundred and fifty dollars for ten volumes?

An editorial board was set up, with Dr. Henry Smith Williams, a well-known popular science writer, as the chief editor and the actual writer at Burbank's dictation. With a battery of helpers, they set up shop in the old Burbank cottage while the Burbank family moved to a new residence across the street. Finally, during the years 1914 and 1915, the monumental work on Burbank appeared. It came to twelve volumes, rather than the announced ten, and thus cost the members one hundred and eighty dollars rather than the one hundred and fifty originally contracted for. The full title of the work was: *Luther Burbank: His Methods and Discoveries and Their Practical Application,* with a note saying that they were prepared "from his original field notes covering more than one hundred thousand experiments made during forty years devoted to Plant Improvement." A special page was inserted at the front of each set carrying a dedication to the subscriber—his name printed in block letters—as an *Honary Member of The Luther Burbank Soiety* and with the signature of the Secretary, Robert John, at the bottom. Burbank's prestige and popularity were being traded on in a grand manner.

It was a handsome job of book-making. The big volumes, bound in maroon cloth, gold lettered, each with a photograph of Burbank pasted on the cover made an attractive and important looking addition to anyone's book shelves. And inside, among the more than thirty-six hundred pages, there was everything about Burbank that anyone but the trained specialist could want to know. His life and all his experiments and productions to date were recorded in simple language. The editor-in-chief succeeded in presenting Burbank in his best possible light to a hero-worshipping public. Besides the text, the volumes contained an extraordinary feature that makes them a joy to any reader or browser to this day. They contained some twelve hundred extraordinarily beautiful full-page color photographs of Burbank's fruits and flowers, each one pasted in by hand. The society went to great expense and pains to achieve excellent color photograph and its reproduction in print, at a time when both processes were in their infancy.

The volumes were a magnificent tribute to Burbank—one that few men ever receive in their own lifetime. They are still exciting, and occasionally a complete set can be found in a second-hand bookstore. Unfortunately, the venture was a financial failure. According to the officers of the Luther Burbank Society or Press (the distinction between them was a vague one) they had spent four hundred thousand dollars by the time the twelve volumes were completed. They had grand schemes for getting back the investors' money and making a big profit in the future. There were to be abridged popular editions, supposedly to be sold to seven million farmers, a textbook edition, a special library edition, foreign language editions, and so on. These and other ventures were to bring in a profit of more than a million dollars. A few months later the whole venture collapsed. The stockholders lost their investment. Burbank had gotten only a portion of the thirty thousand dollars he had been promised, though he did continue to receive some royalties for the rest of his life. Again, people thought they had become members of a Society headed by Burbank himself. Some believed Burbank had deceived them. The whole episode did Burbank's reputation great harm in scientific and intellectual circles.

This was the second colossal failure, in one year, of schemes to make money out of Burbank's name. Both must have been bitter pills to Burbank, but as usual, whether things went well or badly for him, he kept his peace and tirelessly continued his work. He never lost heart, nor did the public lose faith in him.

Two undeniable facts kept Burbank's reputation undimmed, in spite of misrepresentations, speculating promoters, and two big bankruptcies. The first was that Burbank's own honesty and integrity were never questioned. Too many people had known and dealt with him. They found him modest, absolutely sincere, of the highes personal integrity, and a charming, lovable man. The second was that, regardless of exaggerated claims and scientific shortcomings, he was a pioneer in new large-scale methods of plant breeding. The Burbank legend kept right on going.

Chapter 13

In a Glass House

By 1915 Burbank was a world figure. On the wall of his study was tacked a quotation from Emerson. It read:

> *If a man write a better book, preach a better sermon, or make a better mousetrap than his neighbor, though he build his home in the wilderness, the world will make a beaten path to his door.*

Burbank had made better plants than all his neighbors, and the world had come to him. In fact, his chief problem was how to keep himself from being beaten down by those who made a path to his door.

Every day, crowds of people gathered around his

house and gardens. Some merely wanted to catch a glimpse of the great man. Others called out greetings, seeking his attention. Still others stretched out their hands to try to shake his. These were people who had no appointments. Others came in groups by special arrangements through travel bureaus or the local Chamber of Commerce. It was not unusual for Burbank to escort a party of seventy-five or more on a tour of his gardens.

He often asked himself what was he to do? His life was his work and he wanted his work appreciated. But so many people were coming to see him that he felt like a monkey in a cage.

"If I see them all I can't do any work, and if I don't, they are resentful," he complained to his friends.

Burbank found it highly gratifying but terribly irksome to be a celebrity. In one way he liked the crowds outside his garden gates. Their presence bore witness that his life work was a success. He believed that he had devoted all his talents and energies to the service of mankind, and he did want recognition for his aims and achievements.

His livelihood came too, indirectly, from the people who bought his new varieties from nurserymen. It was his public reputation that made the nurserymen so eager to buy his new yearly offerings. Besides, he needed all the income he could get to carry on his ever-expanding experimental projects. It seemed that every year he lived there were more projects, not fewer. But now he was getting older, he tired more easily, and he deplored the time visitors took from the tremendous amount of work that remained to be done.

For this reason he put a sign at the entrance to his grounds reading,

NOTHING FOR SALE:
ALL VISITORS CALL AT THE DOOR.

At the door he had another sign:

ALL VISITORS ARE LIMITED
TO 5 MINUTES EACH
UNLESS BY SPECIAL APPOINTMENT.

Inside the door, for those who got that far, there was an application form to be filled out and handed to one of his secretaries. There were two questions on it: "What is your business with Mr. Burbank? For whose benefit is this interview?" In this way, Burbank tried to cut down the number of people who clamored to see him. Some came for information on how to set up a nursery. Others came to complain that one of his productions, bought from a nurseryman, failed to live up to expectations. Some wanted to tell him about their ideas for new varieties of fruits or flowers. Some even brought him their tired looking house plants to ask him for a diagnosis, as they would take an ailing dog to a veterinarian. There were smart-alecks and bores. But among all the people who flocked to Santa Rosa, there were some Burbank really wanted to see, and whom he enjoyed showing through his gardens. He would go far out of his way to be a gracious host to professors and scientists whose interest and approval he sought. But he liked especially to talk to children and to people who showed a real love for nature and who asked sensible, down-to-earth questions.

His mail was another heavy burden, even though in his later years he had two secretaries to assist him. He was receiving about forty thousand letters a year. One to two hundred letters a day had to be opened, sorted and answered. A printed card was used to answer many of these letters. It read:

> ASK NO QUESTIONS WHICH YOU THINK
> CAN BE ANSWERED ELSEWHERE.
> IF A REPLY IS DESIRED WHICH
> REQUIRES MORE SPACE THAN A
> POSTAL CARD AFFORDS,
> ALWAYS ENCLOSE $5.

The press found him good copy and reporters never left him alone for long. Everyone, too, who wanted to advance himself in the public eye knew that a visit with Burbank would bring the photographers and reporters. This led him to remark, sadly and cynically, that many of the visits he had from celebrities he owed to publicity promoters. "Why else," he asked, "would so many have visited an old crank like me?"

Every mail brought requests for his endorsement of something or other, invitations to speak to various organizations, announcements that he was being awarded this or that gold medal for outstanding service to California, the United States, or the world in general.

The summer and fall of 1915 brought an especially heavy influx of visitors to Santa Rosa. The great Panama-Pacific Exposition, celebrating the opening of the Panama Canal, was being held in San Francisco. Hundreds of thousands of people from all over the world visited the fair, and many of these considered Burbank to be one of its exhibits. People were thought to have missed something if they traveled all the way to California without seeing Burbank and the gardens from which so many fabulous plants had come. A stock phrase they used to get past his secretaries was "I've come a long way to see Luther Burbank." He discovered that this might mean the fifty miles from San Francisco or the seven thousand miles from Australia.

Among the visitors to the Exposition were many famous people, and a few times Burbank even left his work to meet them. Once he went into San Francisco to meet the King and Queen of Belgium. Another time he journeyed to Sacramento at the invitation of Mr. and Mrs. Henry Ford and Mr. and Mrs. Thomas Edison who were making a stopover there. A Sacramento railroad worker recorded that when he heard that the Edison-Ford party and Burbank were to arrive, he rushed to the dispatcher's office shouting: "You'd better step out here a minute. You are going to see something you will never see in your life again—the three biggest men in America, all at once."

The Edisons and Fords stayed one night with Burbank at Santa Rosa, and to his delight they wanted to know everything about his plants and experimental program.

In the short time they were together Burbank and Edison found common features in their work. They agreed that the first task of an inventor was to know exactly what he wanted, whether it was a certain kind of fruit or a new kind of electric light bulb. The next was to search among existing materials for what came closest to meeting their aims. Then, they agreed, came the hard, patient and dogged work of getting from what they had to what they wanted.

It was interesting to Burbank that what Ford most noticed and admired was the size of his operations and the division of labor, whereby great numbers of plants would be handled at the same time and put through the same operation, such as transplanting, fertilizing, grafting, pruning, and the like. Edison's attention was on the inventive side of Burbank's work. Ford was especially interested in the mass-production phase of his work.

There were many other distinguished visitors to Burbank and his gardens that same year. Ignace Paderewski, the great pianist who was later to become Premier of Poland, stopped over during a concert tour of the West Coast. The famous opera singers, Madame Schumann-Heink and Nellie Melba visited him, as did Harry Lauder, the popular Scottish singer of ballads and comic songs. There were others in whose esteem Burbank basked and whose acquaintance he cherished. Ambassadors and maharajas, botanists, physicists and poets stopped by, but it was the famed blind Helen Keller whose visit Burbank knew he would never forget. He delighted in her sensitivity to the smells, textures, and tastes of the products of his garden.

Yet all the while, with the crowds at the gates and visitors coming and going, the work went on. Ben Franklin's adage, "early to bed. . . ." was a life-long habit with Burbank, though he told his friends that he was more certain of the health and wealth it had given him than he was of the wisdom. He was usually in bed at nine o'clock, often as much for the opportunity to think as to sleep. He got up at dawn, and was soon at work at his Sebastopol trial orchard, seven miles away. The California sun was very hot, and he had to make every minute count to get through by noon. Scores of different kinds of fruit were ripening on thousands of young trees.

He had to observe them all, for size, shape, color, and taste—a job he let no one else do for him.

He examined the ripening fruit, sampling hundreds for their taste, texture, consistency, size of pit, and other qualities he was seeking to strengthen, develop or eliminate. With intense concentration he made on-the-spot decisions, having his assistants mark the trees that were to be removed and consigned to the frequent bonfires. They were the ones which failed to meet his demands.

Among the plum trees the work went more slowly, especially on one group of twelve trees on which some five hundred varieties of grafts were growing. He had to select the best of these for further propagation and remove the others to make room for new grafts.

Flowers, too, had to be examined. Lilies, poppies, evening primroses, daisies and other flowers were selected for qualities desirable to the home gardener.

Although agile and sprightly, and extraordinarily vigorous for his age, by noon Burbank was thoroughly tired. He drove home for lunch, knowing that his assistants had plenty of work to last them through the afternoon.

One afternoon during the summer of 1915, he had an appointment with a party of apple specialists, members of the American Pomological Society, which had arranged for its annual convention to be in San Francisco at the same time as the Exposition. They had brought along a man whom they introduced as Walter L. Howard, Professor of Horticulture at the University of California. Burbank affably showed the group through his gardens, explaining his latest creations and the experiments under way.

After an hour, the society members had to leave, but Professor Howard admitted he was able to stay longer, and Burbank immediately invited him to do so. Together the two men walked across the street to Burbank's home. Here Burbank showed his guest the records of some apples he was particularly interested in, along with notes of other fruits under trial. Leaving his visitor to browse among his notes, he attended to other business with his secretaries. Soon he returned and took his visitor back to the gardens.

Outside the house, which occupied a corner lot, the professor noticed that both sides of the intersecting streets were lined with cars. A great crowd was milling around, looking over the picket fence. But Burbank continued to show his visitor trees and shrubs as if the crowd did not exist. The male secretary kept trying to get his attention, but Burbank brushed him off, as if to say "Don't bother me, I can talk to this visitor as long as I please."

Then Professor Howard noticed a big, black, shiny limousine parked outside, with a man in a morning coat and top hat surrounded by other men in formal dress.

He tried to excuse himself, remarking that it looked as if some distinguished visitors wanted to see Burbank, and that he was taking too much of his time. Burbank, not even turning to look around, said "Oh, that's only the Governor of Pennsylvania; let him wait!"

Then he turned to his guest and asked: "But you people, why don't you come to see me more often?" It hurt him that unlike the public generally, university scientists paid relatively little attention to his work.

Chapter *14*

A Lovable Man

Burbank was good-looking at forty and strikingly handsome at seventy. He usually wore a gray or black suit of excellent quality, stiff shirt, collar, and cravat— even while working in the gardens. He is said to have had as many shoes as a fashionable lady and enough gloves to open a shop. When he passed in his open buggy, his bicycle, or later, driving a Ford, people thought he looked like a clergyman or a professor.

Everyone who met Luther Burbank was touched by his charm and graciousness. There may not have been "magic" in his creations, but there was magic in his personality. The famous plant explorer, David Fairchild, after meeting Burbank said, "You feel his kindly and gentle spirit, and before you know it you love him." Scientists who questioned his theory and even deplored his methods could not help but conclude, after a visit to Santa Rosa, that Burbank was "an altogether lovable person." That is why it has been said that no one who knew Burbank, even casually, could ever be completely objective with regard to his work. His personality radiated simplicity and his profound confidence in the value of the work he was doing.

As he grew older, his hair turned gray and whitened. He became slightly stooped. But he still walked with a firm step and kept his unusual agility. Even when he was seventy-six, an observer watching him grafting or pollinating in his gardens said, "his hands were like dragon flies above a pool." And at that age he could still vault a gate with one hand on the rail. Burbank explained it this way: "It's because my body is no older than my mind, and my mind is adolescent. It has never grown up. It never will, I hope. I'm as inquisitive as I was at eight." All his life he kept this freshness and wonder and interest in everything around him.

When Burbank was just past forty he married a woman from Denver he had met and fallen in love with on a cross-country trip. It was an unfortunate marriage. She was jealous of his mother who had lived with him since his early years in California, and she did not like his sister Emma. She yelled at any children who came near the garden, and one evening slammed a door in

Burbank's face and gave him a black eye. Later that night she threatened to shoot him. For two years he lived in a little room above a shed in his gardens where he could lock himself in. After seven years of this impossible marriage, Burbank sued for divorce and won it.

He lived a bachelor life until he was sixty-seven when he married one of his secretaries, Elizabeth Waters, who had worked in his office for two years. The newspapers reported that this was his first marriage—so private had he kept his personal life. A tragedy of Burbank's life, perhaps, was that there were no children from either marriage, for he loved children above all else.

Burbank expressed more than a fond memory of his own childhood surroundings when he wrote:

> *Every child should have mud pies, grasshoppers, water bugs, tadpoles, frogs, mud turtles, nuts, trees to climb, brooks to wade, water lilies, woodchucks, bats, bees, butterflies, various animals to pet, hayfields, pine cones, rocks to roll, sand, snakes, huckleberries and hornets, and any child who has been deprived of these has been deprived of the best part of his education.*

Luther Burbank's love of children was an inseparable part of his whole outlook on life and the world. Children, he thought, were amazingly variable, the most pliable and most precious product of all the ages. None of the plants he ever worked with, nor the machines that man invented, were as pliable and changeable as children.

"But do we encourage," he would ask, "their different temperaments, inclinations, strengths and weaknesses? Instead, we pour them all into one mould, like

Children always found a welcome in the Burbank garden.

steel wire fed through a pin-making machine." We so standardize them "that you can hardly tell their minds apart."

"Children are so like plants," he often mused. "The heredities of both are long and mixed, he believed, and under certain environments the good or the bad traits are reinforced. Give either an environment which encourages an old, sinister trait, and it comes to the surface. When this happens to plants they have to be weeded out and destroyed. When it happens with people "there is a job for the police department, the insane asylum, or the penitentiary," he once said. The weaklings and the perverse "must be given a proper environment early, and their stronger and better talents and traits and tendencies accented and brought out, so that perhaps the bad characteristics will be submerged or drowned out of the unfortunate."

In the generations after Isaac Newton, many thinkers thought of men as machines, in the manner of the Newtonian universe. Burbank, on the contrary, following Darwin's evolutionary biology, thought of men as plants, products of complicated patterns of heredity and environment, constantly subject to growth and change.

As fame began coming to Burbank, he quietly enjoyed it. "We don't grow up entirely," he told a friend as he explained how he sometimes left the safe door open a bit so that visitors would get a glimpse of some of his trophies and insist on having them shown.

Burbank won fame, but he never made a fortune nor did he try to make one. As Henry Ford explained, Burbank "chose to investigate in a field where the financial returns were very small and hence he remained until the end chiefly dependent upon his own personal effort." Ford noted that Edison had "far greater ingenuity in money-making," for he "pursued lines which held promise of financial reward, so that in a very short while he was able to organize himself into a research and inventing institution."

In any case, Burbank neither organized a business to make money nor did he ever ask for aid from any individual, institution, state, or federal government. Visiting foreign scientists and horticulturists often expressed amazement that no grant had ever been given Burbank by the government. That no grant was given was not any shortcoming of the government but rather an expression of Burbank's own personality.

Everyone agrees that he could have become a fabulously rich man, "the richest in the United States," it was said sometimes. He simply did not consider this an object worth seeking or attaining. He found his reward in his work and its products.

Burbank saw plant breeding not only as a vocation, but a valuable hobby for all classes of people. He would have preferred selling direct to the home gardener and plant lover rather than to nurseries. "I should have preferred it above all others," he said, "and the reason I have as far as I could, pursued it is that it brought me into immediate and direct contact with the people I have found uniformly the highest type in the world: the people who grow things and take a pride in them, and want the best of them, and understand the work involved in producing them."

He saw many ways in which plant breeding as a hobby could improve the people who worked at it. First of all, it combined scientific experimentation with the creative work of the artist. It broadened and deepened one's experience with nature and life. It might even turn out to be of direct economic value, for even on the smallest scale, he felt, there was always the possibility that one may produce a valuable new flower or vegetable. And last but not least, he added, it teaches honesty and devotion to truth. "Nature never lies nor can she be deceived," was a motto with Burbank. Records can be falsified but a plant can't be. It is what it is, and when crossed with another, the progeny will follow nature's laws, not man's fancies. And, as in all scientific work, it is impossible to succeed in plant breeding without the most rigorous observation of what is actually *there*. And so, Burbank believed, men improve themselves in their efforts to improve plants.

Chapter 15

A Home-Spun Philosophy

In the Burbank home in Lancaster, Massachusetts, it was a rule that the family go to church Sunday morning. One member, however, was excused to stay home and prepare the Sunday dinner. It was Luther who most frequently volunteered for kitchen work in preference to going to church.

One day, when he was seventeen, Luther was rambling in the woods when he felt something many New Englanders had felt before him—a religious awakening. He experienced a God of law and of science, an infinite being in harmony with all of nature. From that hour on, he began to dream of a *Religion of Humanity*, a religion of sympathy, kindness, love, peace and health.

During the years that followed, Burbank, occupied with his dreams and his work, kept his religious thoughts to himself. But he read, mostly in bed at night, English and French authors whose views he found sympathetic to his own. He re-read the Bible, especially the New Testament, and found the life of Jesus the most beautiful in history. Jealousy, hatred, greed, war: these were the evils of mankind, together with ignorance and disease, he believed. "Ignorance," he loved to say, "is the one unpardonable sin." Science, he came to think, had done more in twenty years towards conquering disease than all the so-called miracle workers through all the ages.

Over the years Burbank developed a philosophy. Nature is impersonal, he believed. Man is no more important to nature than the mosquito, the rattlesnake or the cactus; neither are we nature's favorites, for nature plays no favorites. Man's superiority, insofar as he has any, lies solely in his intelligence.

To spend a life in "nature's university," Burbank thought, is to see man as nature's highest production, and to see nature as harmonious with man's highest ideals. Emerson and Thoreau, he believed, Agassiz and Beebe, and Darwin above all, had achieved this vision of nature and man working together. He believed that the more man knows about fish, lions, and buttercups, the more he will learn about man and his possibilities.

Burbank hated outworn ideas. "I would swap a

whole cartload of precedents any time," he said, "for one brand new idea." He seemed to think that his famous bonfires of discarded plants was similar not only to nature's destruction of out-worn forms of life but also to man's casting off outworn ideas and customs. And he enjoyed setting off charges of intellectual dynamite to advance men's ideas of their relationship to one another and to nature.

Burbank drew another lesson for mankind from his gardens. This was the desirability of constant hybridization, or the mixing of many different kinds of people. One of the reasons, he believed, for the rapid rise of the United States, was that its people were so thoroughly hybridized. "Hybrids," he liked to say, "are what make the world go forward." Once he received unusual potatoes from an old Wisconsin Indian who wanted him to cross them with others to see if good "half-breed potatoes" might result. This uneducated Indian, he thought, understood the value of hybridization better than many scientists.

Continuing in this strain, he once said that hybrids "give us our inventors and poets, our dreamers and leaders of the earth. And in the plant world they are the fragrant and gracious flowers, the lucious and nourishing fruits, the succulent and meaty vegetables." He added, "Have you ever noticed that the most intelligent, the most loyal, and the most friendly dog is usually a mongrel—a cross between two good strains?"

Biology, however, was not enough. To move forward, man also needed an appropriate environment, one that encouraged his natural love of beauty and his humanitarian impulses. Only then would "man's thoughts be turned from the base destructive forces into the nobler productive ones, which will lift him to higher planes of action toward that happy day when man shall offer his brother man, not bullets and bayonets, but richer grains, better fruits and fairer flowers."

The key to human progress lay in science, Burbank fervently believed. It did not matter whether the scientist's work was closely related to human needs and desires or not. Whether it seemed useless, like searching for the North Pole or naming a new species of fish, it was still a contribution to our knowledge. Burbank believed, with Francis Bacon, that "knowledge is power." Bacon's *New Atlantis* sought to picture science organized in the service of mankind and had anticipated the kind of work to which Burbank had given his life. Science is the dynamo, Burbank felt, that can "give added possibilities to life."

But while the work of all scientists could be put to human use, Burbank's ideal man was one who combined science with a love of humanity—the scientist "whose research and study and experiments and discoveries are all directed to the end that man may find this old sphere a better and more beautiful place in which to live." Such was Burbank's own personal goal. Believing that he had lived that kind of life, he exclaimed in his last year, "I do not envy any man living!"

Few people, if any, knew how much Burbank had thought in his later years about the age-old problems of the philosophers. Outwardly, he was the same kindly, tolerant man he had always been to friends, neighbors and associates. Inwardly, he was boiling over with ideas about man and his world, some of which were published only after his death. Society has evolved, he thought, as the whole plant and animal world has, towards higher levels. But it still has a long way to go. "Man today is far from free," he wrote. Men are "slaves yet to war, crime, bigotry, and ignorance—to ancient 'taboos,' superstitions, prejudices and fallacies." Science was aiding mankind because it "has opened our eyes to the vastness of the universe and given us light, truth and freedom from fear."

Applying these broad philosophical ideas to the American scene in the 1920's, Burbank saw the vast productive capacity of the United States being frittered away in "useless waste." Too few people, he thought, were engaged in exploiting "the inexhaustible forces of Nature," and far too many in exploiting their fellow beings.

Burbank had become more unorthodox than his public worshippers and perhaps even he himself knew. Then the storm broke, and he became the unfortunate center of a religious hurricane.

Chapter *16*

The Ordeal: Trial by Press

Frank Piazzi never forgave the press and himself for the part they played in the ordeal that led to Burbank's death. The trouble started with what seemed an innocent telephone call from the editor of an Oakland, California, newspaper. Piazzi was a young Santa Rosa newspaperman who was brought up in a house across the street from Burbank's experimental gardens and who was now working for that newspaper. On his way to and from school, the young Piazzi had seen Burbank working amidst his flowers every day for years, and often, as a boy, he had stopped to talk to him, marveling at the man's patience and tirelessness. Burbank often took the time to explain to the boy some of the qualities he was trying to get out of the plants he was working with. Later, as a young reporter, Piazzi had often interviewed Burbank or brought others to whom he gave interviews.

The newspaper editor, in his telephone call to Burbank, asked if Burbank would comment on a recent interview with Henry Ford, published in a national magazine, concerning Ford's beliefs about immortality. The Oakland editor thought it would make a good feature to compare the beliefs of two famous Americans.

Luther Burbank promised to grant an interview to the reporter he knew from early school days. After the interview had been written, Burbank called in his wife to look it over. Mrs. Burbank recognized how controversial the subject was and deleted some of her husband's statements. "They are too liable to start undesirable arguments," she explained, "and too many people will write to Luther to take issue with him." He's so conscientious that he wants to answer all of them. I try to save him from getting too much mail."

The interview appeared the next day, January 19, 1926, in the Oakland *Post*. The press services picked it up and sent it throughout the country. Then the storm broke, and a daily avalanche of mail began to descend upon him.

For several years Burbank had been worrying about the growing efforts of certain religious leaders to hinder or prevent the teaching of evolution in the nation's schools. "Those who would legislate against the teaching of evolution," he said, "should also legislate against gravity, electricity, and the unreasonable speed of light."

The very kind of thing Burbank feared came to pass with the trial of a Tennessee biology teacher, John T. Scopes, under the new state act forbidding the teaching of evolution in Tennessee schools. Burbank feared that more such laws would be passed which would hinder the advance of science, therefore he had spoken out bluntly in his interview.

Henry Ford, in his interview, had told of his belief that the individual would never die but would live on in another world or in some sort of reincarnation in this one. Luther Burbank said in his interview that there was no scientific justification for "a theory of personal resurrection or reincarnation of the individual."

He added to this the fateful words: "All religions of the past and probably all of the future will sooner or later become petrified forms instead of living helps to mankind."

Letters started arriving by the hundreds; more interviews were sought and given. Burbank wanted people to understand him. He did not want to harm anyone or hurt anyone. He just wanted people to understand his belief that the accepted religion of the day was no more final than the accepted science, and that both had to learn to live together. In one of these interviews he called himself an "infidel" and declared that Christ had been an infidel, too, in his day, "because he rebelled against the prevailing religion and government."

The news went round the world. Some eight-thousand newspapers and magazines spread the word of his "anti-religious" beliefs. Correspondents camped on his doorstep. Photographers were behind every tree and hedge. A group of women in Santa Rosa formed a prayer circle to ask God to forgive him.

A number of ministers invited Burbank to speak in their churches and present his views. He accepted an invitation to speak in San Francisco at the first Congregational Church. The church had two thousand seats, but more than twenty-five hundred people were present, in spite of a terrific downpour.

A few close friends attended with fearful misgivings. Burbank, they knew, was terribly shy and very reserved. He had dreaded public speaking as a student at the Lancaster Academy in Massachusetts sixty years before, and had never felt at ease before an audience. He began to speak, slowly, the audience hanging on every word.

"I love everybody," he began, "I love everything. I love especially to look into the deep, worshipful, liquid eyes of Bonito, my dog, whose devotion is as profound as life itself. But better yet, I love to look into the fearless, honest, trusting eyes of a child who so long has been said by theologians to be conceived and born in sin and pre-damned at birth."

His voice was clear and thin, yet it filled the huge church as the vast congregation listened, fascinated by the frail, white-haired handsome man they had known about all their lives.

"I love humanity," he continued, "I love flowers, trees, and all the works of nature. What a joy life is when you have made a close working partnership with nature, helping her to produce for the benefit of mankind!"

"My mother," the speaker continued, his voice becoming firmer as he gained confidence from the apparent friendliness of the audience before him, "who lived to the ripe old age of ninety-seven years, used very often in my boyhood and youthful days to say, 'Luther, I wish you to make this world a better place to live in than it was before you lived.' I have unfailingly tried all my long life to live up to this standard. I was not told to believe this or that or be damned. Let us have one world at a time and let us make the journey one of joy to our fellow passengers."

California's "grand old man," as he was affectionately called, finished his one and only sermon with an appeal to the congregation to distinguish between true religion, which consisted of love and reverence for man and nature, and the false religion of "bigots and hypocrites."

Then the service was over. The First Congregational Church pastor congratulated Mr. Burbank, and the vast audience pushed forward to shake his hand, deeply moved by his message of love for humanity. It took the greater part of an hour till the last of the thousand who had waited to convey their appreciation had been able to shake his hand.

Thus the man who had often told his friends that his right to his personal belief was sacred had been driven to express his convictions before the nation and the world. He was not only defending his life's purpose but all that he had come to believe in the course of half a century of work. He who thought that "the greatest happiness in the world is to make others happy," was also fond of saying "the next greatest is to make them think." This time he might not be making too many happy, but under the pressure of defending himself, he was certainly making men think.

The next day, February 1, 1926, the storm really broke. Burbank's Sunday "sermon" was carried round the world. Headlines spread the word and editorials in countless papers discussed America's new-found "infidel." His correspondence jumped into the thousands. His telephone rang day and night. Reporters camped on his doorstep. Telegrams poured in. Cables came from as far as Australia and New Zealand.

A clergyman friend, the Reverend Frederick W. Clampett, stayed with Burbank throughout this stormy period, helping him with the letters. Some nine thousand of them came in two months. Each morning the floor was piled high with the incoming mail, all of which was gone through. Some writers praised him; others rebuked and scolded. There were days when Reverend Clampett, who understood Burbank and deeply respected his convictions, wanted to burn them all in a big bonfire such as those Burbank made every year of his discarded plants and trees. But among the letters were hundreds from young people who were troubled with personal doubts. These Burbank read carefully and put aside for a personal response.

"This is heartbreaking," Burbank murmured sometimes as he lingered over a letter, often with tears in his eyes. Many letters came from workers in coal mines and steel mills that warmed his heart with their friendliness and such frank statements as, "let's have the truth at all costs." Then there was the sad letter from a Baptist minister who was removed from his pulpit for a sermon endorsing Burbank's statement.

There were the hostile letters, too, such as one from Abilene, Kansas, which said: "One Bryan is worth a million Burbanks to any world, and the Bible will be doing business when you and your flowers are blowing down the years." But the ones that hurt and angered him most were those that told him to stick to his own field of plants and not to intrude into the field of theology.

Meanwhile the newspapers canvassed everybody who was anybody in search of opinions to keep the controversial fire burning. Scientists, clergymen, public figures were asked for their views, while Sunday after Sunday Burbank's disbelief in immortality and orthodox religion was attacked or defended in innumerable sermons. Henry Ford, whose views had started the whole conflict, came to his friend's defense and made newspaper headlines from coast to coast, such as:

FORD DEFENDS BURBANK'S FAITH; SURE HE BELIEVES IN HEREAFTER.

This was not exactly the kind of defense Burbank wanted.

The New York Times editorialized on the misfortune that Burbank had begun talking about things about which he is no more an authority than anyone else. "His personal opinions as to immortality and the nature of God," the *Times* said a week after the famous sermon, "have gained some attention merely because he long since proved himself better able than most people to select one promising seedling from ten thousand."

Meanwhile, the townspeople of Santa Rosa, where the great religious thunderstorm centered, went their way as usual. The dignified, somewhat aloof, but affable man, who had for several generations been a veritable Santa Claus to their children, had come to be accepted just as he was. To them he was so good, so kindly, and had brought so much fame to their town, that they simply wouldn't think badly about him no matter what he said. His own, almost "saintly" life seemed to them sufficient.

The mayor paid tribute to Burbank's years of service.

Thus it was that on Burbank's seventy-seventh birthday, March 7, 1926, while congratulatory telegrams were pouring into Santa Rosa from all parts of the world, virtually the whole city turned out to honor him. Festivities were held at Burbank Memorial Park and, as had been the custom for many years, all the school children paraded and their spokesmen, together with city officials, formally greeted their aging hero. Burbank, appearing to be in the best of health, simply commented that he was looking forward to another year of hard work in his experimental gardens.

This, unfortunately, was not to be. As his friend Frederick Clampett described it, the strain of the controversy and heavy mail was telling on him as the days and weeks passed. It was bad enough that the man who had lived out of doors all his life was confined within four walls trying to answer mail.

During the night of March 26th he suffered a slight heart attack. His doctors said it was from "overdoing things," but the newspapers carried the story that he was ill "from a nervous reaction due to criticisms of his public utterance on the destiny of man."

Daily press bulletins went over the nation's wires, giving every change in Burbank's condition together with his pulse rate, respiration, and other details. Only Presidents and movie idols had ever had such attention. His doctors said "his eagerness for work is making him hard to treat." On the night of April 11, Burbank died. Over the country the Associated Press wire ran: "Luther Burbank passed on to the great adventure of a hereafter in which he had no faith."

Final services were held three days later under his beloved Cedar of Lebanon in his own garden. This had been his favorite resting place and it was here he had asked to be buried, with no headstone and no marker—the tree his only monument.

It was less than three months after the fateful interview. During these months he was in the public domain, living on the press services' wires and the newspaper headlines, the pulpit and the lecture platform, and it proved too much for him.

Chapter *17*

The Burbank Heritage

The first question people asked after Burbank's death
was: "What will become of Burbank's experimental gardens?" His Sebastopol farm was his largest and most important one, but the Santa Rosa gardens were the ones that
were best known to the public. Thousands of people had
journeyed to Santa Rosa every year to see them. In the
popular mind they had become a kind of public institution, and it was inconceivable that they might not always
be maintained. A proposal to do away with them would
have been as shocking as a proposal to tear down the Sta-
tue of Liberty or the Washington Monument.

The announcement of Burbank's death raised a second question: "Who is going to carry on his work?" Peo-

ple wondered if he had left trained successors. Was there any kind of organization to continue improving plants on the scale he had done for a half a century?

Before he died Burbank had requested Stanford University to take over his gardens and to make provision for their maintenance. Immediately after his death, Mrs. Burbank offered to transfer to the University his experiments, planting plans, and existing experimental trees and plants, together with ample land and equipment for research and experimentation. Some of the University trustees were interested. David Starr Jordan, former President and Chancellor, long a scientific supporter and friend of Burbank, was strongly in favor of the plan. Some of the trustees were hostile, and the majority were indifferent. About one million dollars would be required to maintain the land, and this money was never raised.

In the latter part of 1927, Mrs. Burbank sold exclusive rights to all uncompleted experiments and all existing seeds and bulbs—everything but the land itself and the buildings—to the famous, century-old Stark Brothers Nurseries of Missouri. But everyone asked, what about the gardens themselves? What would become of these?

Mrs. Burbank gave up the new tract and house in Santa Rosa and moved back into the original Burbank home in the gardens where her husband had first attained fame. Some portions of both gardens were cut up for building lots. Thoughtful people were alarmed lest Burbank's "Garden of Enchantment," or "The Inspired Garden," as it had often been called, be lost forever. On December 30, 1927, *The New York Times* carried an editorial on the subject. "The shade of the master," it ran, "as it haunts the Cedar of Lebanon under which he is buried in his garden, must be reminded of the ingratitude of a people to whose state Burbank helped to bring deserved fame." And the editors asked plaintively, "What will future visitors say when they learn that California was too poor to save two acres of garden which had become famous throughout the world?"

Six years later, in 1933, the Santa Rosa Junior College took over the world's most famous garden, with Mrs. Burbank retaining occupancy of the residence just behind the Cedar of Lebanon tree. At last the garden was being maintained as a public memorial. In 1939, during the Golden Gate International Exposition in San Francisco, 50,600 persons signed the garden visitor's book.

This arrangement, however, proved to be unsatisfactory. In the mid-1950's the city of Santa Rosa set up a Burbank Commission with Mrs. Burbank as one of its members. On August 16, 1955, the Commission presented the whole property to the city. By a strange coincidence, almost on the same day, a delegation of Russian farmers, headed by Acting Soviet Minister of Agriculture, Vladimir Matskevich, paid a surprise visit to the neglect-

Scores of visitors daily pass through the Burbank gardens.

ed gardens. They brought floral wreaths for Burbank's grave and an honor medallion for Mrs. Burbank. The eyes of the world were now on Santa Rosa as it undertook at last to make the garden into an appropriate permanent memorial.

Finally the grounds were reconstructed, and Burbank's work was highlighted by grouping some of his most spectacular creations. Every day of the year, throngs of visitors from all parts of the world file reverently along the paths, admiring the great smooth slabs of the spineless cactus, the beautiful Paradox Walnut tree, the Shasta daisies, and scores more of Luther Burbank's unique creations.

There are two other physical memorials to Burbank. One is near Lancaster, Massachusetts, where he was born. The old homestead was demolished in World War II to make way for Fort Devens, a training area for infantry assault troops. The stately elms were bullet riddled, and only a few scattered bricks remained to mark the spot where his birthplace stood.

Years passed and the site was ignored. In 1959, a Lancaster Catholic priest, Father John O'Brien, spoke of Burbank and a memorial to him to the General who commanded the Fort. The General was interested and asked to see the place where Burbank was born. When shown the spot, he ordered a half-acre area, where the home had once stood, set aside and put in good order. A small concrete obelisk, bearing a bronze plaque commemorating the site, was erected, and school children placed a wreath of Shasta daisies at its base.

The other monument is in Michigan. Five years before the old brick homestead was destroyed for military purposes, Henry Ford had the wooden wing in which Burbank was born taken apart and reassembled in his historic Greenfield Village in Dearborn. It was furnished as in the period of Burbank's birth, even including his cradle. Ford also moved to his historic village Burbank's little garden office that stood in a corner of his Santa Rosa plot. There, with some of Burbank's original record books, it stands near Thomas Edison's famous old laboratory moved from Menlo Park, New Jersey, and the bicycle shop from Dayton, Ohio, in which Wilbur and Orville Wright constructed their first airplanes.

Memorials could be maintained and monuments built, but there was no one person to carry on Burbank's work. The public was shocked to learn this, having taken it for granted that he was not an individual working alone, but a kind of institution that would automatically perpetuate itself. While Henry Ford admired Burbank's mass production methods, and Edison saw close resemblances in their inventive work, Burbank had failed in one thing in which these others had eminently succeeded. He had failed in the building of an organization. All three men were pioneers in their respective fields, but for reasons of personality or temperament, Burbank worked entirely alone. Unlike Edison, Ford, and so many other titans of the age, Burbank never made the transition from the Emersonian individualist to the "organization man" of twentieth century America.

Although Burbank employed many assistants he never hired an expert as a consultant or adviser. Edison, on the contrary, though he began as the same kind of lone

[*180*]

wolf, worked at Menlo Park with a whole team which included mechanics, technicians, and people with highly specialized scientific training. His little organization, it has been said, was a kind of pilot model of later great industrial research laboratories.

If Burbank's work stopped at his death, the kind of work he did has continued and grown through the years, partly as a result of his fame and reputation. But perhaps the greatest incentive to the continuance of his kind of work is to be found in a law, the *Plant Patent Act of 1930,* passed by Congress just four years after his death. This law might be considered the most important memorial to Burbank.

In December, 1929, a congressman from Indiana and a senator from Delaware introduced in the Congress this bill to provide for plant patents. The bill took the form of an amendment to the old U.S. Patent Law, designated to protect the inventor of new machines, instruments, or industrial processes. The new bill added to the section reading: "any person who has invented or discovered any new and useful art, machine, manufacture or composition of matter, or any new and useful improvements thereof," the novel clause, "or who has invented or discovered and asexually reproduced any distinct and new variety of plant . . . not known or used by others in this country before his invention or discovery thereof."

There was some opposition by legislators who had

no idea what inventing new kinds of plants meant. One senator said he did not want to take the responsibility of stopping passage of the bill but that the Senate ought to realize, "what a departure it is from anything we have ever done."

Another senator asked if it was "constitutional" to patent a plant that someone might develop through natural processes. A third said the bill was impractical. "Are we going to lay our hand on nature and say, 'you can go only this way and that way?'"

One senator, who had originally opposed the bill, informed the Senate some days later that he now favored it. What had changed his mind was a new kind of apple. He had bought a hundred trees of this variety and found them so remarkable that he was happy someone had the energy to develop them. "Undoubtedly" the senator said "a similar thing has happened many times. It happened in the experience of Mr. Burbank of California. It does give incentive to horticulturists to find ways of developing fine fruits."

The big nursery companies were in favor of the bill. The Department of Agriculture favored it, and agricultural research stations everywhere registered their support. But the bill was assured passage in the Senate only when telegrams were read from Thomas Edison and Mrs. Luther Burbank. Edison wired: "Nothing that Congress could do to help farming would be of greater value and permanence than to give to the plant breeder the same status as the mechanical and chemical inventors now have through the patent law. There are but few plant breeders. This will, I feel sure, give us many Burbanks."

Mrs. Burbank's message spoke of her late husband's great desire for such a measure to provide incentives for men engaged in creative work with plants. It concluded: "If Mr. Burbank were living I know he would be in the forefront of the campaign to secure protection for other devoted men giving their lives to the service of mankind."

In the House of Representatives some feared the bill would establish a precedent for patents on new varieties of cows or chickens.

"Are seeds included in this act?" asked Representative Fiorello La Guardia of New York. He was afraid someone would plant a field of wheat or some other grain and then find that it was patented and have to plow it all up. Discussion brought out that seeds were exempted, because seeds were formed only as a result of sexual reproduction. The law covered only plants produced from cuttings, layerings, or grafts, and controlled only the selling of new plants produced in similar ways.

After all the explanation, La Guardia still maintained that the bill was "rather novel," adding that "Luther Burbank did very well without protection."

Representative Purnell challenged La Guardia: "Why should a man who invents a mousetrap or a jazz song have protection and enjoy the privileges that the patent system gives him, and a man like Luther Burbank, who spent his life developing new plants, gets nothing?"

"Is there a greater benefactor than the man who produces a new vegetable or a new fruit?" he asked.

La Guardia conceded: "I will go further and state that I consider Luther Burbank the outstanding American of his time."

The Bill passed both houses of Congress and was signed by President Herbert Hoover on May 23, 1930. The very conception of it symbolizes the triumph of Burbank's career. It vindicated the principle to which he had dedicated his life. In 1878, when the starry-eyed young man took a train for California, systematic plant breeding was mostly a dream. Now it was protected by law. The plant inventor had come into his own!

The Plant Patent Law permits the owner of a patent to license growers to propagate cuttings or grafts and to collect a royalty on sales for seventeen years. Not long after the act was passed, $10,000 was paid by a nursery firm for the patent rights to a single plant. In the first two years of the law, the nursery which had bought Burbank's experimental plants patented, in Mrs. Burbank's name, five of his finest plums, which had never before been introduced to the public. In another decade the number of posthumous Burbank patents from the vast experimental crop in his Sebastopol orchards had reached thirty-four.

Today one can go into a nursery, or even a department store, and see roses or tomatoes or apple trees on sale, each with a tag attached, such as this on a rose: *"Tiffany.* Plant Patent No. 1304. Asexual Reproduction of this patented plant without license is prohibited." In the thirty years since the law was passed, more than two thousand plant patents have been issued.

Only one question remained: what had Burbank actually accomplished? How many of his "new creations" were as new as he claimed them to be, and would stand the test of time?

Most of the questions about Burbank's work were answered in the winter of 1945-46 when the periodical *Chronica Botanica* published a double issue on the subject, written by Dr. Walter L. Howard, Professor Emeritus of the University of California, and former Director of its College of Agriculture.

Professor Howard, who had visited Burbank back in 1915 began in 1932 to compile a catalog of Burbank's plant productions. He thought it would be task of a few weeks or months. Instead, it took him ten years.

The following are a few of Dr. Howard's findings: Burbank had introduced over 800 new strains and varieties of plants, including over 250 varieties of new fruits. Some of these new varieties were still offered for sale by dealers after forty years had gone by—four times the average life-history of new varieties. Several strains of his potato were being planted all over the country after seventy years. Of his plums, twenty varieties were still widely grown, not only in California but also in South America, Africa and Australia.

Dr. Howard ascertained that thousands of carloads of Burbank's plums were still being shipped from California each year. With the Shasta Daisy, a completely new race of daisies came into being. Permanent improvements in gladioli, lilies, poppies, roses, and scores of other flowers have resulted from Burbank's work, not to mention some sixty-nine new varieties of cactus.

Professor Howard wanted the unvarnished truth about Burbank, and approaching his subject "with none too gentle hands," he sought to tear away the glittering tinsel his worshippers had covered him with, and the dark veils which schemers and detractors had cast over him.

Professor Howard summed up Burbank's life and accomplishments as follows:

And behold a pristine figure emerges that is every inch a man of worth, a man of original ideas: a man with a definite mission in life, fully capable of standing on his own feet as a lone worker in the field of science.

And, Professor Howard continued:

It is impossible to evaluate Burbank's accomplishments with finality, but they were many and diverse, some direct, some indirect. Delving into details, the historian is amazed at the multiplicity of things that one man could do.

SUGGESTED READINGS

The following books are the main source of our information about Burbank. He himself wrote almost nothing, but he provided the material for several of the works listed.

Luther Burbank: His Methods and Discoveries and Their Practical Application, under the editorial direction of John Whitson, Robert John and Henry Smith Williams. 12 volumes, New York and London, Luther Burbank Press, 1914-1915.

Partner of Nature. Edited and transcribed by Wilbur Hall, New York, 1929. (A one volume summary of the 12 volume work above.)

The Harvest of the Years. By Luther Burbank with Wilbur Hall, Boston and New York, 1927.

New Creations in Plant Life: An Authoritative Account of the Life and Work of Luther Burbank. By W. S. Harwood, New York, 1906.

The Scientific Aspects of Luther Burbank's Work. By David Starr Jordan and Vernon Lee Kellogg. San Francisco, 1909.

Plant Breeding: Comments on the Experiments of Nilsson and Burbank. By Hugo De Vries. Chicago, 1907.

The Early Life and Letters of Luther Burbank. By Emma Burbank Beeson. San Francisco, 1927.

Luther Burbank: A Victim of Hero Worship. By Walter L. Howard. *Chronica Botanica,* Waltham, Massachusetts, Winter, 1945-1946.

E=M